Inspira... Stories for Kids

Messi, Ronaldo, Mbappe, and Morgan Biographies

By Lucas Martin

About the Author

Lucas Martin is a passionate author in the field of children's soccer, a sports enthusiast, and a passionate children's book author. Visit www.sportsstoriesforkids.com and get FREE access to Lucas's Soccer Skills Starter Kit.

In his books, Lucas shares his passion and knowledge for soccer and the inspiring stories of the greatest soccer players of all time. He turns these lessons into fun and engaging stories that help children develop healthy relationships with themselves, with others, and with soccer.

In his honest and inspiring books, Lucas discusses the benefits of playing soccer and following your dreams. He shares the best practices for helping children develop soccer skills, confidence, teamwork, and sportsmanship. He also guides you to discover, create, and become who you want to be.

A child of British parents, Lucas speaks Spanish and English fluently. When he's not on his mission to change the world, he loves to play soccer with his kids, read, travel, and watch soccer games.

Lucas grew up in Buenos Aires, Argentina, where he faced many challenges and difficulties in pursuing his soccer passion. He was inspired by

Messi, who overcame his humble origins and became one of the best soccer players in history. He decided to write in this niche to share Messi's story and values with other children who may face similar challenges and difficulties and to inspire and empower them to follow their passion and achieve their potential.

Lucas lives in Barcelona, Spain, with his wife and two kids, a girl, and a boy, where he enjoys the culture and history of soccer and Messi's career. Besides that, he's a huge fan of hockey, basketball, and football, among other sports.

Lucas drafts books that he would love for his children to read to create self-confident adults filled with a passion for sports and its values.

Disclaimer Notice:

Your Free Gifts

To thank you for your purchase, I'm offering my readers the eBook, *Building Confidence for Kids*, for FREE.

To get instant access, go to: https://www.sportsstoriesforkids.com/freegift

Ready to Raise a Super Confident Kid?

Why this eBook is so essential:

- **Enhance Performance in Sports:** Confidence is critical in sports; it empowers children to believe in their abilities and improves their performance on the field.
- **Growth mindset development:** A confident kid is more inclined towards embodying a growth mindset, meaning they see challenges as opportunities to learn and grow rather than insurmountable obstacles.
- **Long-term Life Skills:** Building confidence helps children develop essential skills such as independence, problem-solving, and decision-making.

This eBook is valued at $5, but it is completely free for you!

And that's not all!

You will also receive a comprehensive collection of parenting eBooks that I've personally curated. These five volumes include parenting guides, self-esteem building, rules and discipline, and practical parenting tips.

This special book bundle is valued at $14,99. But, of course, it is free for you!

Grab the free book and the parenting book bundle for the best advice on raising a confident child.

But there is more! Of course, there is a special gift for your kid too!

Free Gifts For Your Kid

1.   FREE E-BOOK:

"The Young Player's Playbook: Winning Strategies for Soccer Success: From Basic Drills to Big Dreams – A Soccer Star's Roadmap for Ages 6 to 12"

The ultimate guide to developing soccer skills and confidence-building on and off the field!

2. Lionel Messi's Journey:

An Inspirational Digital Timeline Poster

This poster will be a daily source of inspiration!

For instant access, go to:
www.sportsstoriesforkids.com/freegift

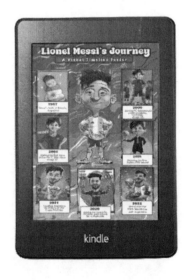

Contents

About the Author   2

Your Free Gifts   6

Free Gifts For Your Kid   9

Introduction   1

Chapter 1: The Messi Effect: All About Lionel Messi   8

Before the Field 10

Battling the Odds 12

Friends and Foes 14

Playing Style and Skills 15

Can You Play Like Messi? Of Course, You Can!   17

Beyond the Field 19

Footprints of Legends 21

Messi Fun Facts 23

What Did We Learn? 24

Messi Soccer Star Quiz 25

Bonus Game: Messi Match..........................30

Chapter 2: The King of Skills: All About Cristiano Ronaldo   **32**

Before the Field.............................34

Battling the Odds...........................36

Friends and Foes............................39

Playing Style and Skills 42

Can You Play Like Ronaldo? Of Course, You Can!   42

Beyond the Field............................44

Footprints of Legends......................47

Ronaldo Fun Facts...........................49

What Did We Learn?.........................50

Ronaldo Soccer Star Quiz..................51

Bonus Game: Ronaldo's Fun Fill-in-the-Blank Adventure! 55

Chapter 3: The Lightning Bolt: All About Kylian Mbappe   **58**

Before the Field.............................61

Battling the Odds 62

Friends and Foes 68

Playing Style and Skills 70

Can You Play Like Mbappe? Of Course, You Can! 72

Beyond the Field 74

Footprints of Legends 75

Mbappé Fun Facts 78

What Did We Learn? 79

Mbappé Soccer Star Quiz 79

Bonus Game: Mbappé Word Search Adventure 85

Chapter 4: Alex Morgan 88

Before the Field 91

Battling the Odds 93

Friends and Foes 96

Playing Style and Skills 97

Can You Play Like Morgan? Of Course, You Can! 99

Beyond the Field 101

Footprints of Legends 103

Morgan Fun Facts 105

What Did We Learn? 105

Morgan Soccer Star Quiz 106

Bonus Game: Alex Morgan Scavenger Hunt
....109

Conclusion   **112**

What Did We Learn? 117

What Can You Do Now? 119

Reflection Questions 121

Thank You 127

Chapter "Good Will"   **129**

Join the Adventure with "Inspirational Soccer Stories for Kids Series"   **131**

Answer Key   **133**

Mbappé Soccer Star Quiz 135

Bonus Game: Mbappé Word Search
Adventure 136

Morgan Soccer Star Quiz...........................136

References **138**

Introduction

Max loved soccer. His bedroom walls were plastered with posters of his favorite stars and he never missed a match on TV. Even his toys became players in his make-believe games. But most of all, he cherished playing the game. Every day, rain or shine, he'd sprint outside with his friends to kick the ball around.

One sunny afternoon, Max raced across the grassy field, his soccer ball bouncing eagerly at his side.

"Watch out, Max! You're going too fast!" called out his friend, Emily, from the sidelines.

But Max was too caught up in the excitement of the game to heed her warning. With a determined grin, he dribbled past defenders, his eyes fixed on the goal.

Suddenly, as he went for a daring shot, Max stumbled over the ball and crashed to the ground with a loud thud.

"Ouch!" he yelped, clutching his ankle in pain.

Emily rushed over, her eyes wide with concern. "Are you okay, Max? Let me help you up."

Max winced as he tried to stand, but his ankle felt too sore to bear his weight. Tears welled up in his eyes as he realized he couldn't continue playing.

"I-I think I hurt my ankle," he murmured, his voice shaky.

Emily placed a comforting hand on his shoulder. "It's okay, Max. Let's get you some help."

Together they limped off the field, Emily supporting Max as they made their way to the sidelines. Max's coach hurried over, concern etched on his face.

"What happened, Max? Are you hurt?" he asked, kneeling down beside them.

Max nodded, his lower lip trembling. "I fell and hurt my ankle," he explained, trying to hold back tears.

The coach looked at Max's ankle carefully and frowned. "It looks like you might have sprained it, Max. We'll need to get some ice on it right away."

As the coach helped Max, Emily stayed by his side, trying to say things that would make him feel better.

"Don't worry, Max," she said, giving him a bright smile.

The coach quickly wrapped Max's ankle and reassured him, "You'll probably be back playing in no time, Max." Then, with a nice pat on the shoulder, he went to check on the other kids, leaving Max and Emily alone for a moment.

"See? It's not so bad, right?" Emily asked.

Max sighed. "Yeah, but this is what I was always afraid of, getting hurt while playing soccer."

Emily nodded, understanding. "I get it. Injuries can be scary, but they're just part of the game. Remember what the coach said about coming back stronger?"

Max nodded, feeling a bit better. "Yeah, you're right. I guess it's just frustrating."

"It is, but you'll bounce back, Max. Just like all those players you admire," Emily encouraged, echoing the coach's words about setbacks not defining them.

Max managed a small smile. "Thanks, Emily. I guess I just needed someone to talk to about it."

"Hey, at least you can play because you're a boy. I'm a girl," Emily said with a sad voice.

Max frowned. He knew this wasn't fair, either. "Yeah, it's not fair. Girls can play soccer just as well as boys."

Emily nodded. "Exactly! It's just a stereotype that soccer is only for boys. Girls can be amazing players too."

"Yeah, definitely! And we should all be able to play without anyone thinking it's weird or different," Max agreed, his determination growing.

"Exactly, Max! We need to break those stereotypes and show everyone that soccer is for everyone, no matter their gender," Emily cheered, feeling better.

Max grinned, "You're right, Emily. Let's show them what we're made of!"

Then the coach returned, noticing Max and Emily deep in conversation. "What are you two talking about?" he inquired, his curiosity piqued.

Max glanced at Emily before replying, "We're talking about how we're afraid of getting hurt in soccer and how unfair it is that it's usually seen as a boys' sport."

The coach nodded thoughtfully, understanding their concerns. "I see. Well, you're not alone in feeling that way. Many players, even famous ones, have had to deal with injuries and stereotypes."

"Really?" Emily asked.

The coach nodded. "Absolutely. Take Lionel Messi, for example. He faced challenges and injuries throughout his career, but he never let them hold him back. And as for stereotypes, many women soccer players, like Alex Morgan, have been breaking them their entire career, showing the world that talent knows no gender."

Max and Emily exchanged looks, impressed by the coach's words. "Wow, I didn't know that," Max said, feeling inspired.

"Yeah, that's pretty cool," Emily agreed, newfound hope filling her. "Can you... can you tell us more about them?

"Sure," The coach smiled at them. He sat down with them and said, "Where should we start?"

Imagine being able to bend a soccer ball like Messi, outmaneuver defenders like Ronaldo, or sprint down the field as fast as Mbappe. This book takes you on a journey through the lives of these soccer giants!

Dive into the stories of Lionel Messi, Cristiano Ronaldo, Kylian Mbappe, and Alex Morgan to discover the life lessons that propelled them from young dreamers to global icons. Uncover the secrets of their success, the challenges they faced, and how they used their passion for soccer to build self-confidence, dedication, and resilience.

Just like Emily and Max, you might love soccer but think about things that are holding you back. Good thing this book is here to help!

Maybe you worry you can't relate to the experiences of world-class soccer players. Don't worry! This book shows that every soccer star started just like you—playing with friends and dreaming big.

Are you afraid of getting hurt? It's okay! This book talks about how even the best players face injuries but come back stronger.

And, it's frustrating when soccer books act like soccer is just for boys, right? Well, this book isn't like that. It shows how girls can be amazing soccer players! Soccer is for everyone, no matter where you're from or what you look like. This book includes all kinds of soccer experiences so every kid can see themselves in the story.

And if you aren't the biggest fan of reading, don't dismiss this. We have made these stories super fun. We have filled this book with exciting stories and real soccer action. It shows the ups and downs of playing soccer without making it too simple or too dramatic. I mean, it's not just about learning; you want to have fun too! This book balances teaching you cool soccer stuff with keeping you entertained.

So, get ready to kick off an awesome adventure with Emily, Max, and a bunch of soccer stars!

Chapter 1: The Messi Effect: All About Lionel Messi

"Day-to-day motivation isn't a problem for me."

-Lionel Messi

"You know," the coach began, "lots of famous soccer players had to deal with tough challenges, just like you two."

The coach sat down with Max and Emily, who were still feeling a mix of frustration and worry.

Max and Emily exchanged curious glances. "Like who?" Emily asked.

The coach smiled and said, "Well, let me tell you about Lionel Messi. When Messi was a kid, he loved soccer just like you do. But he had a big problem. He had a growth hormone deficiency, which meant he wasn't growing like other kids his age. The doctors said he might not get much taller."

Max's eyes widened. "Really? How did he keep playing soccer then?"

"It was really hard for him. Some people thought he might not be able to play at a high level because he was so small. But Messi didn't give up. He and his family found a way to get him the treatment he needed, even though it was expensive and not easy. His unyielding spirit showed that nothing is impossible."

Emily leaned forward, intrigued. "So he kept playing even though it was hard?"

"Exactly," the coach said. "Messi's love for the game and his determination to succeed helped him overcome his challenges. He trained even harder and worked on his skills every day. And look at him now... he's one of the best soccer players in the world."

Max felt a surge of inspiration. "Wow, if Messi can do it, maybe we can overcome our challenges too."

Emily nodded, feeling a newfound hope. "Yeah, we can be strong like Messi."

The coach smiled, seeing the spark of determination in their eyes. "That's the spirit! Remember, every great player has faced obstacles. What matters is how you face them and keep going."

...

If you're looking for the perfect role model to show you amazing soccer skills and teach you to be super brave and not scared of getting hurt, then Lionel Messi is the one for you! Messi is incredible! He shows us that anyone can be a star, no matter what. He's not just amazing at soccer; he also shows us how to work hard and never give up. Messi proves that with determination and courage, you can achieve your dreams. So, if you want to learn from the best and be inspired to be your best, Messi is the ultimate hero!

Before the Field

On June 24, 1987, in Rosario, Argentina, little Leo Messi was born. But right from the start, life wasn't all sunshine and rainbows for him. When he was just a wee lad, around 10 years old, doctors diagnosed him with a growth hormone deficiency, but Messi didn't let that stop him. He was determined to play soccer, and nothing was going to stand in his way!

So, when he was about 13, he did something really brave. He packed up his bags and moved all the way from Argentina to Spain to join FC Barcelona's youth academy. Now, that's like moving across the world for your dreams! But you know what? It was totally worth it!

Fast forward a bit to 2003. Messi's only 16 years old, but guess what? He makes his debut for the Barcelona first team! Can you believe it? A 16-year-old playing with the big guys! And not long after, in 2005, he scored his first goal for Barcelona in a game against Albacete. Talk about making a splash!

But here's the thing: Messi wasn't just some ordinary player. Nah, he was a soccer prodigy! He was dribbling past defenders like they were standing still, scoring goals left and right, and just blowing everyone's minds with his talent.

Battling the Odds

"You'll never be a great soccer player if you're so small!"

When Lionel Messi heard someone say this, he was very sad.

He grew up in a small town in Argentina and loved playing soccer more than anything else in the world. But Lionel had a special challenge... he was shorter than most kids his age because of his growth hormone deficiency.

But, even when people would make fun of him or say he couldn't do it, Lionel would say to himself, "I'll show them what I can do!"

Determined to chase his dreams, Lionel practiced soccer every single day. He dribbled the ball through the streets of his town, imagining himself playing in big stadiums with cheering fans.

One sunny day, a coach saw Lionel playing and was amazed by his skills. He said, "Wow, you're really good! Would you like to join our team?" Lionel's eyes lit up with excitement as he replied, "Yes, I would love to!"

As Lionel grew older, he faced many challenges because of his size. But every time someone doubted him, he would say, "I may be small, but I have a big heart and even bigger dreams!"

Eventually, Lionel's hard work paid off, and he became one of the best soccer players in the world. He showed everyone that no matter how small you are, with determination and courage, you can achieve anything you set your mind to.

And whenever someone asked him how he did it, Lionel would simply smile and say, "I never gave up, and I never stopped believing in myself. And neither should you!"

Aside from his hormone deficiency, Lionel Messi had some tough times on his journey to becoming a soccer star. One big challenge was leaving his family when he was 13 to go play soccer in Spain. It was hard being away from home, but he wanted to follow his dream.

Messi also had to deal with injuries. Sometimes he hurt his muscles or broke his bones, which meant he couldn't play for a while. But he worked hard to get better and kept going.

Messi was also under pressure to do well. Lots of people watched him play and expected him to be amazing every time. Despite it all, he stayed focused and tried his best.

Even with these challenges, Messi never gave up. His love for soccer and his determination helped him become one of the greatest players ever.

Friends and Foes

Lionel Messi had some big games against other top players like Cristiano Ronaldo. They often faced off in matches between Barcelona and Real Madrid, which got fans really excited. They played in tournaments like La Liga and the Champions League, where they both showed off their skills and tried to outdo each other.

Messi had great friendships with his Barcelona teammates, especially Xavi Hernandez and Andrés Iniesta. Together, they won lots of trophies, including the Champions League in 2009, which was a really special moment.

His coaches, like Pep Guardiola, played a big part in Messi's success. Guardiola's smart tactics and leadership helped Messi become even better.

Messi also looked up to other famous players, like Ronaldinho and Diego Maradona. They inspired him to be the best he could be. When Messi scored an amazing goal against Getafe in 2007, it reminded people of Maradona's famous goal, which Messi thought was pretty cool. These players and moments helped shape Messi into the incredible soccer player he is today.

Playing Style and Skills

Messi's playing style is so cool and unique. He's super-fast and can change direction in the blink of an eye. And his dribbling skills? Oh boy, they're out of this world! It's like he's dancing with the ball, making it do whatever he wants!

Messi's signature move, the Messi lift, is especially fascinating. It's flawless precision and flair as he effortlessly lifts the ball over defenders' heads, leaving them stunned and helpless. Watching Messi execute this move is like watching a magician pull off a trick!

Messi's mastery of the chop cut is mesmerizing. Featuring quick changes in direction, Messi pulls it off with finesse every time. He uses it to leave defenders in the dust, slicing through their defense like a hot knife through butter!

Messi's game-changing stop and turn technique allows him to go from full speed to a sudden stop and change direction in an instant. It's like he's playing chess while everyone else is playing checkers!

But wait, there's more! Messi's dribbling style is legendary. He moves with such grace and agility, like he's dancing with the ball. He keeps it glued to his feet, making it impossible for defenders to get a touch. It's no wonder they call him the dribbling maestro!

And let's not forget Messi's incredible ball control technique. His first touch looks like poetry in motion as he brings the ball under his control with ease. Whether it's a pass, a shot, or a dribble, Messi's ball control is second to none.

So, there you have it! Lionel Messi's playing style and skills are a sight to behold. From the Messi lift to his dribbling mastery, Messi is truly a soccer wizard on the field!

Can You Play Like Messi?
Of Course, You Can!

Let's break down each of Lionel Messi's signature moves:

★ **Messi Lift:**
- ○ Start by approaching the ball at a moderate speed.
- ○ As you near the ball, use your non-dominant foot to lightly touch the ball, guiding it upwards.
- ○ At the same time, quickly lift your dominant foot off the ground and angle it slightly downward.

- As the ball rises, use the inside of your dominant foot to flick it up and over the defender.
- Finally, accelerate past the defender and regain control of the ball on the other side.

★ **Chop Cut:**
- Begin by dribbling towards the defender at a controlled pace.
- As you get closer, plant your non-dominant foot firmly on the ground.
- Use the inside of your dominant foot to make a quick, sharp cut across the ball's path.
- Immediately push off with your non-dominant foot and accelerate in the new direction.
- Keep your body low and balanced to maintain control as you leave the defender behind.

★ **Stop and Turn:**
- Approach the defender at full speed, dribbling the ball slightly ahead of you
- Just before reaching the defender, plant your non-dominant foot firmly on the ground.
- Use the inside of your dominant foot to quickly stop the ball by placing it on top of the ball.
- Simultaneously pivot your body in the opposite direction, using your non-dominant foot as the pivot point.

- Push off with your non-dominant foot and accelerate away from the defender in the new direction.

Practice these moves regularly to master Messi's mesmerizing skills and become a soccer wizard on the field!

Beyond the Field

You might be wondering… when Messi's not busy scoring goals and breaking records, what does he do?

Well, for starters, he's a big music lover. You know that feeling when you put on your favorite song and everything just feels right? Messi gets that too! He's got this awesome playlist called "Messi: The Warm-Up," and it's like a glimpse into his musical soul. Now, this playlist isn't your average mixtape. It's got everything from reggaeton to pop to good old Argentine music. Messi's got some serious taste!

Picture this: Bad Bunny blasting through the speakers followed by Karol G, and then some classic hits from Mexican artists like Carin León. He's got songs that pump him up before a game, help him focus, and some that just make him feel good. From Celia Cruz to Selena and a sprinkle of English pop hits by Rihanna and Coldplay, Messi's playlist is as diverse as his playing style.

In addition to dominating the soccer field and curating killer playlists, Lionel Messi is all about his family. He's married to his childhood sweetheart, Antonela Roccuzzo, and they have three adorable sons: Thiago, Mateo, and Ciro. Talk about a full house of love and laughter!

But there's more to the Messi household. They've got some furry friends too! Messi and Antonela are proud pet parents to Hulk and Senor Hulk. Yup, you heard that right, two dogs adding warmth and love to the Messi clan.

When Messi isn't busy being a loving husband and dad, he's hanging out with his friends, just like any other guy. Whether it's grabbing a bite to eat, watching a movie, or even hitting the arcade for some friendly competition, Messi knows how to have a good time with his pals.

And let's not forget about Messi's love for gaming. When he's not training or spending time with his family, you might catch him unwinding with a controller in hand, diving into some virtual adventures. From FIFA to Fortnite, Messi's not afraid to show off his gaming skills when he's off the pitch.

Oh, and did I mention his soft heart? Messi's not just about soccer and music; he's passionate about giving back to the community. Whether it's donating to hospitals, helping out kids in need, or supporting various causes, Messi's always ready to lend a helping hand.

So, there you have it, Messi's not just a soccer superstar; he's also a music aficionado, a family man, a gamer, and a philanthropist. He's a superhero, on and off the field!

Footprints of Legends

Alright, let's explore why Lionel Messi is an absolute legend in the world of soccer! We know he had a strong start in his early years when he joined the youth team of his local club, Newell's Old Boys, at the age of just six. But his big break came when he moved to Spain at the age of 13 to join FC Barcelona's renowned youth academy, La Masia, in 2000.

Messi's talent was undeniable, and he quickly rose through the ranks at Barcelona. In 2004, at the age of 17, he made his first-team debut for Barcelona in a friendly match against FC Porto. Just a year later, in 2005, Messi became the youngest player ever to score a goal for Barcelona in a league match. His breakthrough moment came in the 2005-2006 season when he became a regular starter for Barcelona and scored 14 goals in 26 league appearances.

One of Messi's most memorable performances came in the 2009 UEFA Champions League Final against Manchester United. In that match, Messi scored a brilliant header to help Barcelona secure a 2-0 victory and claim their third Champions League title. His performance earned him the Man of the Match title and solidified his status as one of the best players in the world.

Messi's incredible talent did not go unnoticed, and he began receiving recognition and awards early in his career. In 2005, he won the FIFA World Youth Championship with the Argentine national team, showcasing his potential on the international stage. He also won his first Ballon d'Or award in 2009, becoming the first Argentine player to win the prestigious honor.

Throughout his career, Messi has achieved numerous milestones and broken countless records. He has won a record-breaking seven Ballon d'Or awards, cementing his status as one of the greatest players of all time. Messi has also won numerous league titles, domestic cups, and UEFA Champions League titles with Barcelona.

One of his most famous goals came in a match against Getafe in 2007. This "Hand of God" goal was done with the hand. It was very similar to the goal that Diego Maradona scored with his foot in the El Clásico match against England. Messi's performances in El Clásico matches against Real Madrid are also legendary, with countless memorable goals and moments.

Messi has represented Argentina in multiple FIFA World Cup tournaments and Copa America competitions. Although he has yet to win a World Cup with Argentina, Messi has led his team to the finals of the tournament, showcasing his leadership and skill on the international stage. He has also won the Copa America with Argentina, ending a long drought for the national team in 2021.

Lionel Messi's journey from a young boy with a dream to a global soccer superstar is a testament to his unparalleled talent, determination, and dedication to the sport. His legacy will continue to inspire generations of soccer players and fans for years to come.

Messi Fun Facts

1. Tiny but Mighty: Did you know Messi was really small when he was a kid? He needed special treatment to help him grow, and now he's one of the best soccer players in the world!
2. Doggy Love: Messi has a giant dog named Hulk! Hulk is a big, fluffy dog, and they love

playing soccer together. Imagine having a dog who can play soccer!

3. Sweet Tooth: Messi loves food, especially sweets! His favorite treat is alfajores, which are yummy cookies filled with caramel. He even eats them before games sometimes!

4. Sleepyhead: Messi used to sleep with a soccer ball when he was a kid. He loved soccer so much that he didn't want to be away from his ball even when he was sleeping!

5. Record Breaker: Messi holds the record for the most goals scored in a calendar year. In 2012, he scored 91 goals! That's like scoring a goal every four days for a whole year!

What Did We Learn?

★ Dream big and work hard, just like Messi! No matter where you start, if you believe in yourself and keep practicing, you can reach your goals. Messi didn't have it easy growing up, but he never stopped dreaming, and look where he is now! So, let's dream big and work hard, just like Messi did!

★ Don't let setbacks stop you! Sometimes things don't go the way we want them to, and that's okay. Messi faced tough times and injuries too, but he didn't let them stop him. Instead, he got back up, kept going, and became even stronger! So, if things get tough, remember Messi's story and keep pushing forward. You can do it!

★ Girls and boys can play soccer! Soccer is for everyone, no matter who you are. But sometimes people say that soccer is only for boys, and that's not true! Girls can play soccer just as well as boys. So, let's break those stereotypes and show everyone what we can do on the field!

★ Let's have fun and play with all our heart, just like Messi! Soccer is about more than winning; it's about having fun, being passionate, and giving it your all. Messi loves playing soccer because it brings him joy and excitement, and that's how it should be for all of us! So, let's forget about winning or losing and focus on enjoying the game, just like Messi!

Messi Soccer Star Quiz

Are you ready to test your knowledge about one of the greatest soccer players of all time? Get ready to dive into the world of Lionel Messi with this fun trivia quiz! From his early career to his record-breaking achievements, see how much you know about the legendary Argentine soccer player. Let's kick off the quiz and see if you can score a goal with your Messi knowledge!

What is Lionel Messi's full name?

a) Lionel Andrés Messi

b) Lionel Javier Messi

c) Lionel Diego Messi

d) Lionel Pablo Messi

Which club did Messi join at 13 years old?

a) FC Barcelona

b) Real Madrid

c) Manchester United

d) Boca Juniors

How many Ballon d'Or awards has Messi won as of 2022?

a) 4

b) 6

c) 7

d) 8

In which year did Messi make his professional debut for FC Barcelona?

a) 2001

b) 2003

c) 2005

d) 2007

What is Messi's jersey number at Paris Saint-Germain?

    a) 7

    b) 10

    c) 9

    d) 30

Which country is Lionel Messi from?

    a) Brazil

    b) Argentina

    c) Spain

    d) Portugal

What is Messi's preferred position on the field?

    a) Goalkeeper

    b) Defender

    c) Midfielder

    d) Forward

Which of these awards has Messi NOT won?

a) FIFA World Cup Golden Ball

b) UEFA Champions League Top Scorer

c) Copa America Golden Boot

d) Olympic Gold Medal

What is the name of Messi's wife?

a) Antonella Roccuzzo

b) Shakira

c) Irina Shayk

d) Georgina Rodriguez

How many children does Messi have?

a) 1

b) 2

c) 3

d) 4

Bonus Game: Messi Match

Welcome to the Lionel Messi Matching Game! Join us as we explore the remarkable moments and milestones in the career of the soccer playing icon, Lionel Messi. From his unforgettable goals to his historic achievements, let's match each description with the corresponding event in Messi's illustrious journey. Get ready to match and marvel at the magic of Messi!

Instructions:

Match each description with the correct event or achievement in Lionel Messi's career

Event or Achievement		Year
1) Scored his first professional goal for FC Barcelona		a) 2004
2) Won his first Ballon d'Or award		b) 2005
3) Broke Barcelona's all-time scoring record		c) 2009

4) Scored a hat-trick against Real Madrid in El Clásico	d) 2011
5) Led Argentina to victory in the Copa America	e) 2012
6) Became Barcelona's youngest player to score in La Liga	f) 2014
7) Scored his 500th career goal for Barcelona	g) 2015
8) Named as Barcelona's captain	h) 2016
9) Won his first UEFA Champions League title with Barcelona	i) 2018
10) Signed his first professional contract with Barcelona at age 17	j) 2021

Chapter 2:
The King of Skills: All About
Cristiano Ronaldo

*"There's no point in making predictions. It's not worth
speculating because nothing is set in stone and things change
all the time in (soccer). Today there are opportunities that no
one knows if they will come round again in the future."*

-Cristiano Ronaldo

"So, let me tell you about another amazing player, Cristiano Ronaldo. His journey is all about hard work and sheer will."

Max and Emily listened closely, eager to hear more from their coach.

"Cristiano Ronaldo grew up on a small island in Portugal," the coach began. "He didn't have a lot of money or resources, but he had a dream. From a young age, he practiced every single day, always pushing himself to be better."

Emily looked impressed. "So, he worked really hard to become great?"

"Exactly," the coach said. "Ronaldo's dedication was incredible. When he was just 19 years old, he played in the UEFA Euro 2004 final. He scored two goals in that game, announcing his arrival on the world stage. That was a huge moment for him and showed everyone that he was a force to be reckoned with."

Max's eyes widened with excitement. "Wow, at 19? That's amazing!"

The coach nodded. "Yes, it was. Ronaldo's journey to becoming one of the best players in the world shows that with hard work and determination, you can achieve great things. He never let anything stop him from reaching his goals."

Emily smiled, feeling inspired. "So, if we work hard like Ronaldo, we can achieve our dreams too."

"That's right," the coach said, smiling at them. "Every player faces challenges, but with dedication and effort, you can overcome them and reach your full potential."

...

If you're searching for the ultimate role model to teach you awesome soccer skills and inspire you to be super brave and fearless, Cristiano Ronaldo is your guy! Ronaldo is amazing! He shows us that anyone can become a superstar, no matter where they start. He's not only fantastic at soccer; he also teaches us about hard work and dedication. Ronaldo proves that with perseverance and courage, you can reach your goals. So, if you want to learn from the best and be motivated to achieve greatness, Ronaldo is the perfect hero for you!

Before the Field

I want to tell you about someone super amazing... Cristiano Ronaldo! He's one of the best soccer players ever, and his story is really cool. So, let's dive in!

Cristiano Ronaldo was born on February 5, 1985, in a place called Funchal, on the beautiful island of Madeira in Portugal. Imagine living on a tiny island with the ocean all around you! He lived with his mom, dad, and three siblings. His dad, José Dinis Aveiro, worked for a local soccer club called Andorinha. They named him Ronaldo after Ronald Reagan, who was the U.S. President at the time and also his dad's favorite actor.

When Cristiano was just a kid, he loved playing soccer more than anything. He even played with a ball instead of doing his homework! But it wasn't always easy for him. At the age of 15, he found out he had a heart problem that needed surgery. It was really scary, but he was super brave and got better quickly. After that, nothing could stop him!

He started his soccer journey at a small club called Clube Desportivo Nacional in Madeira. Then he moved to a bigger club, Sporting Clube de Portugal, also known as Sporting Lisbon, where he played in their youth teams. He was so good that he made it to the first team in 2002 at just 17! Imagine being a teenager and already playing with the big guys!

Even as a kid, people could see he was special. He was super fast, had amazing skills, and could do cool tricks with the ball. Everyone knew he was going to be a star, and they were right.

Battling the Odds

Cristiano Ronaldo's relentless drive transformed him from a skinny teenager into one of the most physically dominant players in soccer history. His work ethic has inspired millions around the globe.

When Ronaldo was just a boy, he was often teased for being too skinny. "You're too small to play professional soccer," they'd say. But young Ronaldo didn't let that stop him. "I'll show them," he often muttered to himself, his eyes gleaming with determination.

As a teenager, he joined the Sporting Clube de Portugal. He was smaller than most of the players, but he had something many of them lacked: an unwavering dedication to improving himself. Every day after training, while others were heading home, Ronaldo stayed behind. He'd run extra laps, practice his dribbling, and work on his shooting until the sun set. "I have to be the best," he would tell himself over and over.

His coaches were amazed by his commitment. "This boy has something special," they would say, shaking their heads in disbelief. Ronaldo wasn't just practicing; he was transforming his body. He spent countless hours in the gym, lifting weights and building the muscle that would eventually make him a powerhouse on the field.

Ronaldo's discipline extended beyond the physical. He was meticulous about his diet, understanding that what he put into his body was just as important as how he trained it. "No junk food," he'd remind himself, opting instead for lean proteins, fresh vegetables, and plenty of water.

His hard work paid off. By the time he moved to Manchester United in 2003, Ronaldo was no longer the skinny kid from Madeira. He was a force to be reckoned with; his speed, strength, and skill setting him apart from the rest. Teammates and opponents were in awe of his physical prowess.

"How does he do it?" they'd wonder, watching him sprint past defenders with ease.

Ronaldo's dedication to his craft didn't go unnoticed. "Cristiano's work ethic is second to none," said Sir Alex Ferguson, his manager at Manchester United. "He trains harder than anyone I've ever seen. That's why he's the best."

Even as he achieved unprecedented success, Ronaldo never stopped pushing himself. His daily routine was a testament to his discipline. "Success isn't given, it's earned," he would often say. And earn it he did. His body became a symbol of peak athletic performance, inspiring countless fans to follow in his footsteps.

Cristiano Ronaldo's journey from a skinny teenager to one of the fittest athletes in the world is a story of relentless drive, unwavering discipline, and an extraordinary work ethic. His transformation is a powerful reminder that with dedication and hard work, anything is possible.

Believe it or not, being skinny wasn't Cristiano's biggest challenge. Growing up in Funchal, Madeira, Portugal, his family was really poor. His dad, José Dinis Aveiro, worked as a kit man in a soccer club, and his mom, Maria Dolores dos Santos Aveiro, was a cook and a cleaner. Life was tough because they didn't have much money, but they always tried to make sure Ronaldo and his three siblings had what they needed.

When Ronaldo was just a kid, he loved playing soccer more than anything. He was so good that he joined a local team called Andorinha when he was only 8 years old. But things weren't always easy. In 1997, when Ronaldo was 12, he moved away from his family to join the Sporting Clube de Portugal's academy in Lisbon. It was really hard for him because he missed his family so much and sometimes he felt very lonely.

School wasn't easy for Ronaldo either. When he was 14, he got expelled from school because he threw a chair at a teacher who made fun of his Madeiran accent. He decided to focus all his energy on soccer after that. But even then, things didn't go smoothly. When Ronaldo was 15, he was diagnosed with a racing heart, which could have ended his soccer career. He had to have surgery, but he recovered quickly and was back on the field in no time!

Ronaldo's journey was filled with challenges, but he faced them with determination and hard work. He turned every obstacle into a stepping stone, proving that no matter how tough things get, you can always find a way to achieve your dreams if you keep going and never give up!

Friends and Foes

One of Ronaldo's biggest rivals is Lionel Messi, another amazing player. They've had super exciting matches for teams like Real Madrid and Barcelona, and also in big tournaments for their countries, Portugal and Argentina. People all over the world love watching them play against each other!

Ronaldo has played for amazing teams like Manchester United and Juventus. He's known for working super hard and being a great leader. His teammates think he's really cool and look up to him. Coaches always count on Ronaldo to score goals and help the team win. They say he's one of the best players ever!

When Ronaldo was a kid in Portugal, his family and coaches believed in him. His mom, Dolores, cheered him on at every game and told him to never give up. Ronaldo also looked up to famous players like Luis Figo and Zinedine Zidane. They showed him how to play with passion and skill, and he learned a lot from them. Have you ever watched Cristiano Ronaldo in action? He's like a magician with his bag of tricks! Let me tell you about his incredible playing style and skills.

First, let's talk about his signature move: the Stepover Chop! Picture this: Ronaldo's dribbling down the field, and then, whoosh! He swings his foot around the ball, making it look like he's changing direction. But wait! He quickly drags the ball with his foot in the opposite direction, leaving the defenders in a spin!

Then there's the Elastico... it's like something out of a movie! Ronaldo flicks the ball to one side with the outside of his foot, and in a flash, he's gone the other way! It's like he's playing mind games with the defenders, making them think he's going one way when he's actually going the other!

And let's not forget about the CR7 Fake Move. This one's a real showstopper! Ronaldo makes a sharp fake in one direction, and just when you think you've got him figured out, he's off in the opposite direction like a bolt of lightning! It's all about timing and deception, and Ronaldo's got it down to a science!

But wait, there's more! Have you seen Ronaldo's Ball Roll Chop? It's pure magic! He rolls the ball with the sole of his foot, making it look like he's going one way, and then – bam! – he chops with his foot, leaving the defenders in his dust! It's all about precision and timing with this move, and Ronaldo makes it look effortless!

Cristiano Ronaldo's soccer journey is all about exciting rivalries, awesome friendships with teammates and coaches, and the people who inspired him to become a soccer superstar. He's not just a player... he's a hero to kids who dream of playing soccer just like him!

Playing Style and Skills

So, there you have it, Cristiano Ronaldo's playing style and skills in all their glory! With moves like the Stepover Chop, Elastico, CR7 Fake Move, and Ball Roll Chop, it's no wonder he's considered one of the greatest soccer players of all time!

Can You Play Like Ronaldo? Of Course, You Can!

Here's a step-by-step guide on how to perform each of Cristiano Ronaldo's signature moves:

★ Stepover Chop:
   ○ Approach the defender with the ball at your feet.
   ○ Swing your dominant foot around the ball in a stepover motion, as if you're about to change direction.
   ○ Quickly drag the ball with the inside of your dominant foot in the opposite direction.
   ○ Accelerate away from the defender, using your dominant foot's control and speed to move past them.

★ Elastico:
   ○ Dribble towards the defender with the ball on one foot.
   ○ Flick the ball to one side with the outside of your foot, making it look like you're going in that direction.
   ○ Immediately change direction by pulling the ball back with the inside of your foot.
   ○ Accelerate away from the defender, utilizing your quick footwork to create space.

★ CR7 Fake Move:
   ○ Approach the defender with the ball under control.

○ Make a convincing fake in one direction using your standing foot, as if you're about to move that way.

○ Quickly change direction by explosively pushing off your standing foot in the opposite direction.

○ Accelerate away from the defender, capitalizing on the space created by the fake.

★ Ball Roll Chop:

○ Dribble towards the defender with the ball at your feet.

○ Roll the ball to one side with the sole of your foot, making it seem like you're continuing in that direction.

○ Suddenly change direction by chopping the ball with the inside of your foot.

○ Accelerate past the defender, using your footwork and control to maintain possession.

Practice each of these moves diligently, focusing on coordination, timing, and execution. With dedication and perseverance, you can master Cristiano Ronaldo's signature skills and add them to your own repertoire on the soccer pitch!

Beyond the Field

When Ronaldo is not dazzling everyone on the soccer field, he's got so many fun things going on.

First, Ronaldo loves spending time with his family. He's got four adorable kids and a beautiful partner named Georgina. They do everything together, from fun family vacations to just hanging out at home. He's a total family guy, and he loves being a dad more than anything!

But that's not all... Ronaldo also has a bunch of friends he likes to chill with. They might go out for a nice dinner or just relax at home. Sometimes, they play video games! Yep, Ronaldo loves playing video games just like so many of us. Imagine playing FIFA and scoring goals as yourself! How cool is that?

He's also into fitness and health. Even when he's not training, he likes to work out and stay in shape. He's got this amazing gym at home, and he's always sharing tips on how to stay fit and healthy. He even has his own line of fitness products!

And guess what? Ronaldo has a big heart. He loves helping others and is always involved in charity work. He's donated millions to different causes and hospitals, especially for kids. He wants to make sure everyone has a chance to be happy and healthy. For example, he helps Save the Children by raising money and awareness for kids who need help. He also works with UNICEF to support children's rights all around the world. Ronaldo loves making kids happy, so he's part of the Make-A-Wish Foundation, granting wishes for children with serious illnesses. He even donated a lot of money to help hospitals during the COVID-19 pandemic. Plus, he donates to the Red Cross, especially when natural disasters happen, like the big earthquake in Nepal. Ronaldo also supports hospitals that treat kids with cancer. It's clear that Ronaldo has a huge heart, and he uses his fame to help kids and families in need.

Oh, and he loves fashion too! Ronaldo has his own brand called CR7, which includes clothes, shoes, and even fragrances. The name comes from his initials and his jersey number, and it's all about bringing Ronaldo's sleek and modern style to everyone. CR7 clothes are perfect for both sporty activities and looking sharp in everyday life. You can find everything from comfy underwear to trendy jeans and stylish shirts. Ronaldo is really involved in designing these clothes, making sure they look great and feel even better. CR7 shoes are also super popular. They're designed to be both comfortable and fashionable, so you can run around just like Ronaldo or just chill with friends and still look awesome. The shoes come in various styles, from casual sneakers to more formal footwear. And let's not forget about the CR7 fragrances! Ronaldo has a whole line of colognes that smell amazing. These fragrances are designed to make you feel confident and cool, just like Ronaldo. Overall, CR7 is all about bringing a bit of Ronaldo's style and confidence to fans around the world. Whether you're wearing his clothes, rocking his shoes, or spritzing on his cologne, you can feel a little bit like a soccer superstar!

So, when Ronaldo isn't scoring goals, he's being an awesome dad, a great friend, a fitness enthusiast, a fashion icon, and a super kind person. Isn't he just the coolest?

Footprints of Legends

Ronaldo's journey to becoming a legend started when he was just a kid in Portugal. He played for a local team called Sporting Clube de Portugal. His skills were so amazing that people couldn't stop talking about him. Then, in 2003, Manchester United, one of the biggest soccer teams in the world, saw his talent and brought him to England. That was when his superstar journey really began!

One of Ronaldo's breakthrough moments was when he played in the FA Cup final in 2004. He scored an incredible goal and helped his team win the trophy. Everyone was talking about this young, super-talented player. But that was just the beginning!

There were so many matches where Ronaldo showed why he's the best. One unforgettable game was in 2008 when he scored a fantastic header in the UEFA Champions League final, helping Manchester United win the championship. Another jaw-dropping performance was in 2013, when he scored a hat-trick (that's three goals in one game!) against Sweden, securing Portugal's spot in the World Cup.

People quickly noticed how amazing Ronaldo was. He won his first Ballon d'Or in 2008, an award given to the best player in the world! And guess what? He didn't stop there; he won it multiple times afterward, proving he was consistently the best!

Ronaldo's career is packed with highlights. He moved to Real Madrid in 2009 and scored tons of goals, breaking record after record. He won the Champions League four times with Real Madrid! Imagine being the best in Europe four times!

Ronaldo has so many records it's hard to keep track! He became the all-time top scorer for Real Madrid, scoring over 450 goals. He's also one of the top scorers in Champions League history. His speed, skill, and ability to score from almost anywhere on the field are legendary.

There are so many iconic moments! Like the time he scored an incredible bicycle kick against Juventus in 2018. Even the Juventus fans stood up and clapped because it was so amazing! Another unforgettable moment was his long-range free-kick against Portsmouth in 2008. People still talk about that goal!

Ronaldo has shined in many tournaments. He led Portugal to victory in the 2016 UEFA European Championship and the 2019 UEFA Nations League. These were huge wins for his country, and he was the hero in both!

Cristiano Ronaldo is a legend because of his incredible skills, unforgettable performances, and amazing achievements. He's shown the world what you can achieve with talent, hard work, and determination. He's not just a player; he's a superhero on the soccer field!

Ronaldo Fun Facts

1. Crazy Workout: Did you know Ronaldo does over 3,000 sit-ups a day? That takes hours! No wonder he's so strong!
2. Super Speedy: Ronaldo can run as fast as a cheetah! Well, almost. He can sprint at 33.6 kilometers per hour. That's like zooming faster than a race car (okay, maybe not a race car, but you get the idea)!
3. Jumpy Jumper: Ronaldo can jump higher than a basketball hoop! He can leap 78 centimeters off the ground, which is higher than most kids can ever dream of jumping.

4. Healthy Hero: Ronaldo has a super strict diet. He doesn't drink soda or eat junk food, and he loves fish. Imagine eating fish every day!

5. No Tattoos: Unlike many other soccer stars, Ronaldo doesn't have any tattoos. He says it's because he wants to donate blood regularly. How cool and kind is that?

What Did We Learn?

★ Cristiano Ronaldo teaches us a lot about dreaming big and not giving up, no matter what challenges we face. When he was young, he dreamed of being the best soccer player ever. He practiced a lot, even though he didn't have much money. Sometimes things didn't go well for him, like when he got kicked out of school or had heart problems. But he didn't let that stop him. He worked even harder to reach his goals. And guess what? He became one of the best soccer players ever!

★ Another thing Ronaldo shows us is that everyone can play soccer, whether they're a girl or a boy. He thinks everyone should get to play the sport they love, no matter who they are. Ronaldo talks about this a lot and helps support programs that make sure everyone gets a chance to play.

★ Ronaldo reminds us to have fun and put our hearts into what we do. Even though he's a big star, he still loves playing soccer. He plays with so much energy and excitement. Ronaldo wants us to enjoy what we do and give it our all, just like he does.

★ Plus, he teaches us that it's important to be kind and help others. Ronaldo gives a lot of money to charities and visits sick kids in hospitals. He shows us that no matter how famous or rich we are, we can still make a difference in the world by helping those in need.

Ronaldo Soccer Star Quiz

Are you ready to test your knowledge about the legendary Cristiano Ronaldo? Get ready to kick off this fun trivia quiz and show off your Ronaldo expertise! Let's see if you can score a hat-trick of correct answers and become the ultimate Ronaldo champion. Get your game face on and let's dive into the world of one of the greatest soccer players of all time!

What is Cristiano Ronaldo's full name?

a) Cristiano Roberto Ronaldo

b) Cristiano Ronaldo dos Santos Aveiro

c) Cristiano Mario Ronaldo

How many FIFA Ballon d'Or awards has Ronaldo won as of 2024?

a) 3

b) 5

c) 7

In which year did Ronaldo make his professional debut for Sporting Lisbon?

a) 2000

b) 2002

c) 2004

Which club did Ronaldo join after leaving Sporting Lisbon?

a) Manchester United

b) Real Madrid

c) Barcelona

What is Ronaldo's jersey number for the Portugal national team?

a) 7

b) 10

c) 17

How many UEFA Champions League titles has Ronaldo won in his career?

a) 3

b) 5

c) 7

In which country was Cristiano Ronaldo born?

a) Brazil

b) Portugal

c) Spain

What is the name of Ronaldo's fashion brand?

a) CR7

b) Ronaldo Style

c) Fashion Ronaldo

What is Ronaldo's preferred foot for shooting?

a) Right

b) Left

c) Both

Which club did Ronaldo join after leaving Real Madrid in 2018?

a) Juventus

b) Paris Saint-Germain

c) Manchester City

Bonus Game: Ronaldo's Fun Fill-in-the-Blank Adventure!

Are you ready to embark on an exciting journey through the life of one of the greatest soccer players of all time? Cristiano Ronaldo's story is filled with thrilling moments, remarkable achievements, and incredible milestones. Get ready to test your knowledge and fill in the blanks to complete sentences about Ronaldo's extraordinary career!

Instructions:

Fill in the blanks with the correct words to complete the sentences about Cristiano Ronaldo's incredible journey!

Cristiano Ronaldo was born on _____, in _____.

As a kid, Ronaldo loved playing _____ in the streets with his friends.

Ronaldo joined Sporting Clube de Portugal's youth academy at the age of _____.

In _____, Ronaldo made his professional debut for Sporting CP's first team.

In _____, Ronaldo signed with Manchester United and became known for his incredible _____ and _____.

Ronaldo won his first FIFA Ballon d'Or award in _____, while playing for _____.

In _____, Ronaldo transferred to Real Madrid for a world-record fee at that time of _____ million euros.

Ronaldo helped Real Madrid win _____ Champions League titles during his time at the club.

In _____, Ronaldo joined Juventus and continued to showcase his talent in _____.

Cristiano Ronaldo has represented his national team, Portugal, in numerous international tournaments, including the FIFA World Cup and UEFA _____ Championship.

Let the fun begin! See how many blanks you can fill correctly!

Chapter 3:
The Lightning Bolt: All
About Kylian Mbappe

"I am happy, and I am living the life I always dreamed of."
-Kylian Mbappe

"Now," the coach began, "let's learn about Kylian Mbappe and what he can teach us about overcoming difficulties in soccer and the importance of hard work."

Max and Emily listened intently as the coach described how Mbappe had faced challenges on his journey to becoming one of the best soccer players in the world. Coach explained that Mbappe had started playing soccer at a very young age, showing incredible talent but also encountering many obstacles along the way.

"Mbappe didn't have it easy," the coach said. "He had to work extremely hard to improve his skills and prove himself. But even when things were tough, he never gave up. He pushed through injuries, setbacks, and tough competition to become the player he is today."

Max and Emily's eyes widened with interest as the coach continued. "One of the most important lessons we can learn from Mbappe is the power of perseverance. No matter how difficult a situation might be, if you keep working hard and stay determined, you can overcome any obstacle. Mbappe's speed and dribbling skills are a result of countless hours of practice and dedication."

The coach smiled, seeing the inspiration in Max and Emily's eyes. "Mbappe also teaches us the value of hard work. He always trains hard, even when he's already at the top of his game. He never stops trying to improve, and that's what makes him so exceptional."

"So, whenever you're on the field," the coach concluded, "remember Mbappe's story. With perseverance and hard work, you can overcome any difficulty and achieve great things in soccer and in life."

...

If you're looking for the best role model who can show you awesome soccer skills and teach you to be super brave and not scared of getting hurt, then Kylian Mbappe is the one for you! Mbappe is amazing! He shows us that anyone can become a star, no matter what. He's super fast and has incredible dribbling skills, but he also teaches us that hard work and never giving up are the keys to success. Mbappe proves that with determination and courage, you can overcome any challenge and achieve your dreams. So, if you want to learn from someone who never lets anything stop him and always works hard, Mbappe is the ultimate hero!

Before the Field

Let me tell you about Kylian Mbappe and his amazing early life and career! It's like an adventure story!

Kylian Mbappe was born on December 20, 1998, in a town called Bondy in France. His dad, Wilfried, was a soccer coach, and his mom, Fayza, was a handball star for France. With such sporty parents, it's no wonder Kylian became a superstar!

When he was just six years old, Kylian joined the Bondy youth academy, where his dad worked as a coach. Imagine starting your soccer journey with your dad guiding you! Kylian was super fast and had incredible skills, even as a little kid. Everyone at Bondy knew he was something special.

By the time he was 12, in 2010, Kylian moved to Clairefontaine Academy, a famous soccer training center in France. This place is like a magic school for young soccer talents! He spent three years there, learning and practicing hard. He trained with the best young players in the country and got even better at dribbling, passing, and scoring goals.

Then, when he was 15, Kylian joined the Monaco youth academy. This was a big step because Monaco is a top team in France. In no time, Kylian was playing for Monaco's main team. The 2016-17 season was his breakout year. He scored 11 goals and helped Monaco win the Ligue 1 title! People everywhere started talking about this amazing young player from Bondy.

At just 18 years old, Kylian's incredible performances earned him a spot on the French national team in 2017. Playing for your country at such a young age is like a dream come true! And that was just the beginning of his fantastic journey.

Kylian Mbappe's early life and career are like a fairy tale filled with hard work, talent, and big dreams coming true. And guess what? He's still out there, dazzling everyone with his amazing soccer skills! Isn't that the coolest story ever?

Battling the Odds

"What are we going to do?" Kylian Mbappe's father, Wilfried, sighed heavily. "We need to find a way to pay for Kylian's training and travel expenses," he said, looking worried.

Kylian watched from the hallway as his father and mother, Fayza Lamari, talked quietly at their small dining room table. Overhearing the conversation, he felt a pang of guilt. Kylian knew his family faced numerous challenges due to his remarkable talent and potential. From a young age, it was clear that Kylian had a gift for soccer, but nurturing that gift wasn't easy for his family. He knew his family was doing everything they could to support his dream, but it was hard.

Kylian's mother, a former handball player, nodded in agreement. "We've already received some help from the French government, but it's not enough. We might have to make more sacrifices."

Hearing this made Kylian sad. He decided to step in.

"Maybe I can get a part-time job to help out," Kylian suggested as he walked up to his parents, his eyes filled with determination.

"No, son," Wilfried shook his head, smiling sadly. "Your job is to focus on your training and school. We'll manage somehow."

Eventually, the family decided to move to a smaller apartment to cut costs. Kylian and his younger brother, Ethan, had to share a bedroom.

"At least we get to hang out more," Ethan said cheerfully, trying to stay positive.

Despite the cramped living conditions, Kylian remained focused on his training.

"I won't let you down," he often told his parents, his eyes full of promise.

One day, after a particularly grueling training session, Kylian's coach, Antonio Riccardi, pulled Wilfried aside. "Your son is exceptional. I've never seen a talent like his in all my years of coaching. We'll do everything we can to support him."

But even with the coach's encouragement, the financial strain was ever-present. Fayza took on extra work, and Wilfried tried to pick up more coaching gigs.

"We have to keep pushing forward," Fayza said, her voice resolute.

Through it all, Kylian's love for soccer never wavered. He trained hard, aware of the sacrifices his family was making.

"One day, I'll make you proud," he would say, often looking at his parents with gratitude.

And as he continued to grow and develop as a player, the sacrifices began to pay off. Kylian's performances on the field caught the attention of top clubs, and soon, his family's hardships started to ease.

But that was only the beginning of Kylian's struggles.

The more Kylian's star rose, the more his family found themselves under the relentless gaze of the media. The Mbappé household, once a haven of privacy and peace, was now constantly besieged by paparazzi and journalists.

"Why can't they just leave us alone?" Ethan would often complain, frustrated by the flashing cameras that greeted them even on their way to school.

One evening the family sat down for dinner, their small apartment now feeling even more cramped with the weight of constant media scrutiny.

"Kylian, we need to talk," Wilfried said, his voice tinged with concern. "The media attention is getting out of hand. They're hounding us everywhere we go."

Fayza nodded in agreement. "They're not just interested in your soccer anymore, Kylian. They want to know everything about our lives. It's becoming impossible to live normally."

Kylian looked down at his plate, his appetite gone. "I know, Mom. I didn't expect things to get this crazy. But what can we do?"

The situation escalated when Kylian was just 11 years old. Real Madrid, one of the biggest soccer clubs in the world, offered him a contract. The media frenzy that followed was overwhelming. Reporters camped outside their home, shouting questions and snapping photos at every opportunity.

"Kylian, is it true you're going to Real Madrid?" a reporter yelled as the family tried to leave for training one morning. "What does this mean for your future?"

Fayza shielded Kylian with her arm, guiding him towards the car.

"No comments, please. Let us live in peace," she said, her voice strained.

Inside the car, Kylian turned to his parents, his face a mix of excitement and anxiety. "I don't know how to handle this. I'm just a kid who loves soccer."

Wilfried reached over and squeezed his shoulder. "We'll get through this together. Remember, your talent is what brought us here, but we need to stay strong as a family to handle the pressure."

The pressure wasn't just external. There were heated discussions at home about whether to accept Real Madrid's offer.

"It's a great opportunity, but is it the right time?" Fayza wondered aloud one evening. "Kylian is still so young."

Wilfried agreed, adding, "And the media won't leave us alone if he goes. It's already tough as it is."

Ultimately, the family decided that it was best for Kylian to stay in France and continue his development without the intense spotlight that came with such a high-profile move. "I just want to play soccer," Kylian said with a sigh of relief. "We'll figure the rest out later."

Despite the challenges, Kylian remained focused on his passion. The media attention was a constant obstacle, but it also taught him resilience and the importance of family support. "No matter what happens," Kylian often reminded himself, "I have my family by my side. Together, we can face anything."

As Kylian continued to dazzle on the field, his family learned to navigate the complexities of fame. It wasn't easy, but their bond grew stronger, and Kylian's dream stayed alive. The sacrifices they made and the pressures they faced only fueled his determination to succeed and, ultimately, make them proud.

Even though it was tough, Kylian and his family never gave up! They faced money problems and had to share a tiny apartment, but they stuck together. When the media wouldn't leave them alone, they handled it as a team. Even when Real Madrid came knocking, they made the best choice for Kylian's future.

With every challenge, Kylian got stronger and his family's support never wavered. They showed that with love, hard work, and support, you can overcome anything! And guess what? Kylian made his dream come true, and his family was super proud of him.

Friends and Foes

Kylian Mbappé has played in some huge games against the best players and teams in the world. He's had exciting rivalries with players like Erling Haaland, who's also super fast and scores lots of goals. When Mbappé faces off against Haaland, it's always a thrilling battle of skills and speed.

In the Champions League, Mbappé has faced tough teams like Bayern Munich and Barcelona. These matches have shown how good Mbappé is under pressure and how he can score against the toughest opponents.

On the field, Mbappé is great friends with Neymar Jr. They work together to score goals for Paris Saint-Germain (PSG). Their teamwork has helped PSG win lots of games and championships in France.

Mbappé has also learned a lot from his coaches, like Thomas Tuchel and Mauricio Pochettino. They've helped him become an even better player by teaching him new tactics and giving him advice on how to play his best.

As a kid, Mbappé looked up to Thierry Henry, a famous French soccer player. Henry played for France and Arsenal and scored many goals, just like Mbappé dreams of doing. Mbappé also admires Zinedine Zidane, another French soccer hero, for his calmness and skill on the field.

These rivalries, friendships, and heroes have all helped Mbappé become the incredible soccer player he is today. He's shown that with hard work and teamwork, you can achieve your dreams in soccer and beyond.

Playing Style and Skills

Wow, have you ever seen Kylian Mbappé play? He's like a superhero on the soccer field! Kylian's playing style is super fast and exciting. He's really quick on his feet and can zoom past defenders like they're not even there. It's like he's got rockets in his shoes!

One of the coolest things about Mbappé is how he dribbles the ball. He can weave through defenders with fancy footwork and make it look so easy. Sometimes he dribbles so fast that defenders can't keep up with him.

When Kylian unleashes his "step-over" move, it's pure magic! He flicks the ball from side to side, tricking defenders into thinking he's going one way, then zooming past them in the opposite direction.

And when it comes to scoring goals, Kylian is a master. He can shoot with power and accuracy from all angles. He's scored some incredible goals with his lightning-fast shots that leave goalkeepers stunned. When it's time to strike, Mbappé's "curler" shots are a sight to behold. With precision and finesse, he bends the ball around defenders and into the net, leaving goalkeepers grasping at air. It's like he's painting a masterpiece with every shot!

Watch out for Mbappé's "roulette" move! He spins around the ball with lightning speed, leaving defenders spinning in confusion. It's as if he's conjuring a whirlwind that sweeps away anyone in his path.

And his "no-look" passes? They're pure genius! Kylian deceives defenders and mesmerizes spectators by looking in one direction while passing the ball in another. It's like he has eyes in the back of his head!

But Mbappé isn't just about scoring goals. He's also a team player. He's great at passing the ball to his teammates and setting up scoring opportunities for them. He knows exactly when to make a pass or take the shot himself. It's like he sees the whole game unfold before it even happens!

Watching Kylian Mbappé play soccer is like watching a superhero in action. He's got the skills, speed, and smarts to take on any opponent. No wonder everyone loves cheering for him!

Can You Play Like Mbappe?
Of Course, You Can!

Here's a step-by-step guide on how to perform some of Kylian Mbappé's signature moves:

★ **Step-Over:**
  ○ Plant your non-dominant foot next to the ball.
  ○ Use your dominant foot to push the ball to one side.
  ○ Quickly step over the ball with your non-dominant foot, tricking the defender.

○ Accelerate in the opposite direction where you stepped over.

★ **Roulette:**
  ○ Approach the defender with the ball at your feet.
  ○ Step over the ball with your dominant foot, turning your body 180 degrees.
  ○ Use your non-dominant foot to drag the ball behind you in the direction of your spin.
  ○ Accelerate away from the defender after completing the spin.

★ **No-Look Pass:**
  ○ Look in one direction to deceive the defender and draw their attention.
  ○ Using the inside of your dominant foot, pass the ball in the opposite direction.
  ○ Keep your head up and stay aware of your teammates' positions.

★ **Curler Shot:**
  ○ Approach the goal with the ball under control.
  ○ Choose your spot and plant your non-shooting foot next to the ball.
  ○ Use the inside or outside of your dominant foot to strike the ball with a curved motion.
  ○ Aim for the far corner of the goal, using finesse rather than power.

Practice these moves regularly to master them like Kylian Mbappé! Each move requires precision, speed, and quick decision-making, like a true soccer magician.

Beyond the Field

Kylian Mbappe is not just an awesome soccer player, he's also a really fun and interesting person. For starters, he loves spending time with his family. He's super close to his parents, Wilfried and Fayza, and he even has a younger brother named Ethan who he loves playing soccer with. Family time is super important to him!

Now, let's talk about music. Kylian loves listening to music, and he has an epic playlist that he shares with his fans sometimes. You can find it on Spotify by searching his name! He enjoys a mix of French rap and international hits. Some of his favorite artists include Drake, J. Cole, and the French rapper Ninho. Whenever he's getting ready for a big match, you can bet he's listening to some of these tunes to get pumped up!

Kylian also has a bunch of other cool hobbies. He's a big fan of video games, especially FIFA. Imagine playing FIFA and having yourself as a character in the game! He says he used to play FIFA a lot as a kid, and he still loves to play whenever he gets the chance.

Kylian loves cars! He has a collection of super fancy cars like a Ferrari 488 Pista and a Mercedes V Class. He's really into how fast and cool they are. When he's not on the pitch, he might be out driving one of his awesome cars around town.

And guess what? Kylian is also a bit of a fashion enthusiast. He likes to dress stylishly and even works with big brands like Nike. He enjoys looking good on and off the field.

Finally, Kylian is a really kind and generous person. He has his own charity called the "Kylian Mbappe Foundation," which helps kids in France and Africa by giving them opportunities in education and sports. He loves helping others and making a difference in their lives.

So, Kylian Mbappe isn't just a soccer star, he's also a music lover, gamer, car enthusiast, fashion fan, and a really nice guy who loves helping people. Isn't he just the coolest?

Footprints of Legends

Kylian Mbappé is totally a legend, and let me tell you why!

Kylian's journey to becoming a legend is so awesome. When he was only 16 years old, he started playing for AS Monaco, one of the top teams in France. Everyone was like, "Whoa, this kid is incredible!" He made his debut for the first team and broke records left and right. He was Monaco's youngest-ever player and goal scorer... imagine doing that at 16!

But wait, it gets even cooler. Kylian made history in the Champions League, the big league where the best teams play. In February 2017, he scored his first Champions League goal when he was just a teenager! People couldn't believe how fast and skilled he was. He was like lightning on the field, dribbling past defenders and scoring amazing goals.

At the 2018 FIFA World Cup, Kylian Mbappé became the youngest French player to score at the World Cup, a remarkable achievement that showcased his exceptional talent on the international stage. His goal came during the group stage match against Peru, where his decisive strike not only secured a 1-0 victory for France, but also underscored his potential as a future star.

There are so many matches where Kylian showed why he's a legend. Did you know that he scored a hat-trick against Barcelona in the Champions League in February 2021? That was insane! He was unstoppable that day, showing everyone he's one of the greatest.

Right from the start, people knew Kylian was special. He won awards for being the best young player in France and Europe. Even when he played for the French national team in June 2018, he scored goals in big tournaments like the World Cup and the Euros. He's like a superhero on the field, making France proud!

Let me tell you about his major achievements! He's won so many league titles with Paris Saint-Germain and Monaco. He's also broken records for scoring the most goals in the Champions League and for the French national team. And get this, he won the World Cup with France in July 2018! He scored in the final and became a hero in his own country.

There's this one goal he scored against Argentina in the World Cup... it was so amazing! In June 2018, he zoomed past defenders like they weren't even there and scored with style. Everyone was jumping and cheering because he's just that good.

In every big tournament he plays in, Kylian makes a huge impact. Whether it's the Champions League, the World Cup, or the Euros, he always gives it his all. He's won trophies and medals, making him one of the most decorated players of his generation.

Kylian Mbappé is not just a soccer player, he's a legend! He's shown us that with hard work, determination, and a lot of talent, you can achieve your dreams. That's why kids everywhere look up to him and want to be just like him on the field.

Mbappé Fun Facts

★ **Goal Machine:** Mbappé has scored more than 250 goals for his teams, making him a scoring machine on the soccer field!

★ **Fashion Forward:** Mbappé loves fashion! He's known for his stylish clothes and has graced the covers of fashion magazines.

★ **Multi-talented:** Besides soccer, Mbappé is multi-lingual, fluent in French, English, and Spanish. He's a true global superstar!

★ **Animal Lover:** Mbappé has a pet bulldog named Pogba, after his friend and fellow soccer star Paul Pogba. They're both big fans of dogs!

★ **Lightning Speed:** When Mbappé scored an amazing goal against Monaco in 2019, he sprinted from his own half to score, reaching an incredible speed of 38 kilometers per hour (about 23.61 miles per hour)! That's faster than many cars on the road, but... not fast enough. Usain Bolt, the fastest man in the world, reached even higher speeds in his record-breaking sprints. On May 6, 2024, Bolt jokingly challenged Mbappé to a race for charity, showing just how fast and fun Mbappé really is!

What Did We Learn?

★ **Get Started Early:** Just like Kylian Mbappé, start playing soccer early! Whether it's in your backyard, at school, or with friends, the earlier you start, the more you'll improve over time.

★ **Stay Positive after Setbacks:** When things don't go your way, stay positive! Like Kylian, use setbacks as opportunities to learn and grow stronger in your game. Remember, every great player faces challenges.

★ **Play Soccer with Everyone:** Soccer is for everyone! Don't let anyone tell you otherwise. Whether you're a boy or a girl, soccer is a game where everyone can join in and have fun together.

★ **Feel the Excitement:** When you play soccer, feel the excitement just like Kylian does. Whether you're dribbling, passing, or scoring goals, let your love for the game shine through. It's all about having fun and enjoying every moment on the field.

Mbappé Soccer Star Quiz

Think you know everything about one of today's soccer superstars? Get ready to dive into the world of Kylian Mbappé with this thrilling trivia quiz!

From his early career milestones to his record-breaking achievements, test your knowledge about the French soccer sensation. Let's get started and see if you can ace this quiz on Mbappé!

At what age did Kylian Mbappé start playing soccer competitively?

A) 5 years old

B) 6 years old

C) 7 years old

D) 8 years old

At which club did Kylian Mbappé make his professional debut?

A) AS Monaco

B) Paris Saint-Germain

C) Real Madrid

D) Chelsea

How old was Kylian Mbappé when he made his UEFA Champions League debut?

A) 16 years old

B) 17 years old

C) 18 years old

D) 19 years old

In which year did Kylian Mbappé help France win the FIFA World Cup?

A) 2014

B) 2016

C) 2018

D) 2020

Kylian Mbappé became the youngest player to reach 25 goals in the UEFA Champions League. At what age did he achieve this milestone?

A) 19 years old

B) 20 years old

C) 21 years old

D) 22 years old

How many consecutive seasons did Kylian Mbappé win the Ligue 1 Golden Boot award?

A) 2 seasons

B) 3 seasons

C) 4 seasons

D) 5 seasons

Against which team did Kylian Mbappé score his first UEFA Champions League hat-trick?

A) Barcelona

B) Bayern Munich

C) Manchester City

D) Juventus

Kylian Mbappé's father, Wilfried, was also involved in soccer. What role did he play?

A) Football coach

B) Referee

C) Club president

D) Sports journalist

Against which country did Kylian Mbappé make his debut for the French national team?

A) Luxembourg

B) Netherlands

C) Spain

D) England

Besides winning the World Cup, what other record did Kylian Mbappé set during the 2018 tournament?

A) Youngest French goal scorer in World Cup history

B) Fastest hat-trick in World Cup history

C) Most assists in a single World Cup tournament

D) Youngest player to captain the French national team

Bonus Game: Mbappé Word Search Adventure

In this exciting word search game, you'll dive into the world of goals, speed, and championship victories just like the legendary French striker. Grab your pencil, get your thinking cap on, and let's see how quickly you can find all the hidden words related to Mbappé's incredible career. Get set, go!

Instructions:

1. ZGet Ready: Grab a pencil or a colored marker and find a comfortable spot to play.
2. Understand the Grid: Look at the grid of letters in front of you. This grid contains

hidden words related to Kylian Mbappé's career and achievements.

3. Find the Words: Search horizontally, vertically, and diagonally to find the hidden words. Words can be forwards or backwards!

4. Circle or Mark Words: When you find a word, circle it or use a marker to highlight it on the grid.

5. Challenge Yourself: Time yourself to see how quickly you can find all the words, or work with friends and family to see who finds the most words in the shortest time.

6. Have Fun!: Enjoy discovering the exciting words that celebrate Kylian Mbappé's journey from a young talent to a soccer superstar!

Now, grab your pencil, start searching, and have a blast playing the Mbappé Word Search Adventure!

```
q  l  w  s  r  s  b  g  q  f  d  j  n  t  b  w  v  l
n  d  p  c  d  e  t  z  c  v  e  w  k  a  x  m  i  k
z  f  y  x  h  m  c  r  x  o  p  r  i  f  n  q  d  b
z  p  d  w  w  a  p  o  i  b  v  m  h  n  d  f  h  s
m  a  a  z  g  x  m  d  r  k  n  r  m  s  n  i  r  p
b  r  p  d  o  i  v  p  w  d  e  w  j  s  r  e  e  e
c  i  q  m  a  v  t  t  i  b  b  r  a  j  k  i  r  e
e  s  w  k  l  o  p  v  q  o  w  g  f  j  o  i  y  d
k  h  a  t  t  r  i  c  k  a  n  m  r  y  q  k  l  k
o  c  s  e  z  y  x  y  h  x  a  o  y  k  w  y  r  l
q  y  t  o  c  c  u  g  h  q  u  a  v  q  k  c  m  j
c  f  r  a  n  c  e  y  k  u  t  n  j  r  s  k  b  g
```

Find the following words in the puzzle.
Words are hidden → ↓ and ↘ .

hat-trick	winner	skill
champion	record	goal
striker	speed	
france	paris	

Chapter 4: Alex Morgan

"Keep working even when no one is watching."

- Alex Morgan

"Alright, you two, next up is Alex Morgan," the coach said excitedly. "She teaches us so much about being a woman in soccer and what it means to believe in yourself."

"Alex had to deal with a lot of tough teams," the coach explained. "She played really intense games against teams like Canada. Even when things were hard, she never gave up. Her hard work and dedication are really amazing."

The coach talked about her friends and coaches. "Alex is great friends with her teammates, like Megan Rapinoe and Carli Lloyd. They support each other like family. Her coaches, like Jill Ellis and Vlatko Andonovski, helped her get better and better. They made a great team."

"And you know what?" the coach continued, "Alex looked up to other soccer legends like Mia Hamm. They showed her how to play with heart and lead by example. Alex learned to stand up for what's right and inspire others."

"Coach," Max said, "do you think kids like us can really relate to someone as famous as Alex Morgan?"

"That's a good question, Max," the coach replied. "Even though Alex is a world-class player, she started just like you, playing soccer because she loved it. She faced the same challenges you might face, like balancing school and sports, and she worked hard to get better every day. Her story shows that anyone can achieve their dreams if they stay dedicated."

Emily chimed in, 'But what about injuries? Sometimes I get scared thinking about getting hurt."

"Alex has had her share of injuries," the coach said gently. "But she always focused on getting stronger and coming back better. She teaches us that setbacks can be overcome with the right mindset and support from others. Injuries are part of sports, but they don't have to stop you."

"Sometimes it feels like soccer is seen as a 'boys' sport," Max added, looking thoughtful.

"That's something Alex has worked hard to change," the coach said firmly. "She's shown everyone that soccer is for everyone, no matter if you're a boy or a girl. Her success helps break those stereotypes and proves that girls are amazing in sports."

"And coach," Emily asked, "what about books that don't really show how fun soccer is?"

"That can be frustrating," the coach agreed. "But Alex's story is full of excitement and real-life challenges. It's important to find stories that truly capture the spirit of the game and the joy it brings. Alex's journey is not just about soccer; it's about perseverance, teamwork, and believing in yourself."

"Max, Emily," the coach said. "Alex Morgan's story teaches us to be strong, work together, and never give up. She shows that if you work hard and believe in yourself, you can do amazing things. Remember her story as you keep playing and growing in soccer. You can be inspired by her journey and know that you have the potential to achieve great things too."

...

Now you might be feeling just like Max and Emily. Well, Alex Morgan's story will help you, too. She teaches us so much about facing challenges, believing in ourselves, and working hard to reach our dreams. Whether you're worried about relating to a famous player, getting injured, dealing with stereotypes, or finding truly exciting soccer stories, Alex's journey has something for everyone. Read on to learn more and get inspired by how she overcame obstacles and became a soccer legend!

Before the Field

Alex Morgan started playing soccer when she was really young, around 5 years old! She grew up in Diamond Bar, California, and from the start, everyone could see she had something special. When she was in high school at Diamond Bar High, she played on the soccer team and was already outstanding.

In college, Alex went to the University of California, Berkeley, and played for their team, the California Golden Bears. She scored a lot of goals and helped her team win games. It was during this time that she caught the eye of the national team coaches.

One of the coolest things about Alex's early career is that she was part of the U.S. U-20 Women's National Team. In 2008, when she was just 19 years old, she played in the U-20 Women's World Cup in Chile and helped the team win! Imagine being a teenager and winning a world championship... that's amazing!

After college, Alex kept working hard to get even better. She joined the Western New York Flash in the Women's Professional Soccer League and scored a bunch of goals there too. Then in 2011, she joined the U.S. Women's National Team and quickly became one of their key players.

Alex's journey from playing soccer as a kid to becoming a superstar on the world stage is inspiring. She's shown that with talent, determination, and a lot of practice, you can achieve big things in sports and in life!

Battling the Odds

Alex Morgan faced *so many* challenges as a woman soccer player, but her journey was one of resilience and triumph. Growing up, she often heard people say things like, "Girls can't play soccer as well as boys," or "Soccer is a men's sport." These comments bothered her, but they also fueled her determination to prove them wrong.

One day, when Alex was still a teenager playing in a local league, she overheard some boys laughing and saying, "Girls can't score goals like us!" Alex felt a surge of anger and determination. She turned to them with a confident grin and said, "Wanna bet?"

She trained even harder after that, pushing herself to improve her skills every day. Sometimes, after a tough practice where she felt like giving up, she'd call her mom for encouragement.

"Mom," she'd say, "it's so hard sometimes. But I love soccer. I want to show everyone what I can do."

Her mom always knew the right thing to say. "Alex, you're strong and talented. Keep going. You can do this."

As Alex got older, the challenges didn't disappear. She faced critics who said women's soccer wasn't as exciting or as competitive as men's soccer. But Alex never backed down. During one particularly tough game, an opponent tried to intimidate her with rough tackles and harsh words.

"You can't handle this," the opponent sneered.

Alex got up, dusted herself off, and replied calmly, "Watch me."

In the final minutes of that game, with determination burning in her eyes, Alex scored a stunning goal. The crowd erupted in cheers, and her teammates lifted her on their shoulders. It was a moment of triumph, a moment that showed the world what Alex Morgan was made of.

Off the field, Alex became an advocate for women's rights in sports. She spoke out about equal pay and opportunities for female athletes.

"We train just as hard, we play just as well," she told reporters. "We deserve respect and recognition."

Through hard work, courage, and persistence, Alex Morgan became not just a soccer star but a symbol of strength and perseverance for girls and women everywhere. Her journey wasn't easy, but every challenge she faced only made her stronger. And as she looked back on her career, she knew she had overcome obstacles that once seemed insurmountable.

"I'm proud of how far I've come," Alex said with a smile. "And I'm excited for the future of women's soccer."

Unfortunately, this was not the only challenge in Alex Morgan's life. In fact, she had to face lots of tough stuff during her soccer career. One big challenge was when she got hurt. There were times when she couldn't play because of injuries. She had to do a lot of exercises to get better and it was really hard. But she never gave up. She told her coach, "I'll do whatever it takes to get back on the field!"

Another tough thing for Alex was being away from her family and her husband as she had to travel a lot for games and tournaments.

"I miss him," she told her friend, "but he cheers me on from home."

Alex also had to deal with people saying mean stuff about her in the news and on social media. Sometimes they didn't understand how hard she worked. But Alex didn't let it get to her. She focused on playing her best and didn't listen to the negativity.

Even though Alex faced lots of challenges, she always kept going. She showed everyone that with hard work and believing in yourself, you can achieve your dreams, no matter what gets in your way.

Friends and Foes

Alex Morgan has faced off against some really tough teams in big games. These matches are super intense, and it's amazing to see Alex score goals and help her team win. She gets so pumped up playing in tournaments like the World Cup and the Olympics, where she goes head-to-head with these rival teams.

Off the field, Alex is known for being really close with her teammates and coaches. She's not just a great player but also a fantastic leader who cheers everyone on during games and makes sure they all work together as a team. Her teammates, including stars like Megan Rapinoe and Carli Lloyd, are like her soccer family—they support each other through thick and thin.

When Alex was growing up, she looked up to soccer legends like Mia Hamm. Mia showed her how to play with skill and passion, and that inspired Alex to always give her best in every game. These role models taught Alex about the importance of teamwork and standing up for what's right in sports. Now, Alex isn't just a soccer star; she's a role model for kids everywhere who dream of playing like her one day. Her journey shows that with hard work, dedication, and a great team by your side, you can achieve anything in soccer and beyond.

Playing Style and Skills

Have you ever watched Alex Morgan tear up the field? Let me spill the tea on her incredible playing style and skills.

First off, let's talk about her killer move: The Speed Burst! Imagine this: Morgan dashing past defenders like a bullet, leaving them in the dust with her lightning-fast acceleration. It's like she hits turbo mode and zooms straight to the goal!

Then there's the Morgan Spin. It's seriously next-level! Morgan swoops around the ball with a quick turn, confusing defenders who can't keep up. She spins past one, then another, and suddenly she's creating a clear path to score. It's like she's got eyes in the back of her head!

And let's not forget the Header Precision. This move is a game-changer! Morgan times her jumps perfectly, soaring above defenders to redirect the ball with pinpoint accuracy into the net. It's all about technique and timing, and Alex nails it every time!

But hold on tight, because there's more! Have you seen Morgan's Nutmeg Masterclass? It's pure genius! She effortlessly slips the ball through an opponent's legs, leaving them stunned and creating a golden opportunity for her team. It's skill combined with cheeky finesse, and Morgan pulls it off like a true soccer queen!

So, get pumped and ready to learn from the best! Morgan's moves are not just about skill – they're about inspiring us all to bring our A-game every time we step onto the field. Let's kick it like champions!

Can You Play Like Morgan?
Of Course, You Can!

★ **Speed Burst:**
- ○ Start from a standing position or a slight jog, keeping the ball close to your feet.
- ○ Identify open space or a gap between defenders where you want to accelerate.
- ○ Explosively push off with your dominant foot, using short, powerful strides to increase your speed.
- ○ Keep your body low for better balance and control as you sprint past defenders.

- Maintain focus on the ball and your surroundings to adjust your speed and direction as needed.

★ **Morgan Spin:**
- Approach the defender at an angle with the ball under control.
- Use the inside of your dominant foot to quickly spin around the ball, pivoting your body 180 degrees.
- Protect the ball with your body as you turn away from the defender.
- Accelerate into open space or toward the goal, using your non-dominant foot to push off.
- Maintain awareness of surrounding defenders and adjust your speed to avoid challenges.

★ **Header Precision:**
- Position yourself in front of the goal, facing the direction of the incoming cross or pass.
- Time your jump to meet the ball at its highest point, using both hands to guide your ascent.
- Make contact with the ball using your forehead, aiming to redirect it toward the goal.
- Follow through with your jump, ensuring your body remains balanced and stable.
- Land safely and be ready for a potential rebound or follow-up play if the header doesn't score.

★ **Nutmeg Masterclass:**

- ○ Approach the defender with controlled dribbling, keeping the ball close to your feet.
- ○ Observe the defender's positioning and wait for the right moment to execute the nutmeg.
- ○ Use the inside of your foot to gently push the ball through the defender's legs, maintaining control.
- ○ Quickly accelerate past the defender, using your body to shield the ball from retrieval.
- ○ Continue your attack or pass to a teammate while the defender recovers.

These steps teach us the tips behind each of Alex Morgan's signature moves, helping you practice and improve your soccer skills on the field.

Beyond the Field

Did you know Alex Morgan has a super fun life off the soccer field? She's married to Servando Carrasco, who is also a professional soccer player. They met in college at the University of California, Berkeley, where they both played soccer and fell in love. They're like a soccer power couple!

Alex and Servando have a cute dog named Blue. Blue is a fluffy and energetic pup who loves playing fetch and going on walks with Alex and Servando. Sometimes, Blue even joins Alex in training sessions, chasing after the soccer ball like a little athlete!

When Alex isn't training or playing games, she loves spending time with her family and friends. She's really close to her parents, Michael and Pamela, who have supported her soccer career from the beginning. They come to her games and cheer her on like the ultimate fans!

When she's not kicking goals, she loves listening to music and has a really cool playlist! She likes to listen to a mix of upbeat pop songs that pump her up before games, like Miley Cyrus' catchy tunes and Billie Eilish's awesome beats. She even has some throwback songs from the 90s that she jams out to with her friends. You can find her playlist on Apple Music by searching her name!

Besides music, Alex has lots of hobbies that she enjoys. She's really into reading books about strong women and inspiring stories. She loves going to the beach and surfing with her friends and family... Imagine Alex catching waves like a pro! She's also a big fan of yoga and practices it to stay flexible and relaxed.

In her free time, Alex likes to travel to new places and try different foods. She's been to so many cool countries around the world because of soccer, like France and Japan. When she's at home, she enjoys cooking and trying out new recipes, especially healthy ones that keep her in top shape for the next game.

Alex Morgan isn't just a soccer superstar; she's a fun-loving person who enjoys life to the fullest. Whether she's scoring goals on the field or chilling out with her favorite music, she's always bringing energy and positivity wherever she goes!

Footprints of Legends

Let me tell you why Alex Morgan is a total legend! She's like a superhero on the soccer field and her journey to the top is so inspiring!

Alex started making waves when she was really young. She played soccer with so much passion and skill that everyone noticed. One of her breakthrough moments was when she joined the U.S. Women's National Team in 2010. She was super young but already showing she could score goals like nobody's business!

One of her most iconic goals happened in the 2012 Olympics. It was the last-minute goal against Canada in the semifinals! Alex leaped up high and headed the ball into the net, winning the game for Team USA. People went crazy cheering for her!

Alex has had so many significant matches and performances that it's hard to count! She's won Olympic gold medals and helped Team USA win the FIFA Women's World Cup in 2019. Imagine playing in front of millions of people and still scoring amazing goals!

She's won tons of awards too, like being named U.S. Soccer Female Athlete of the Year multiple times. And get this... Alex was even inducted into the U.S. Soccer Hall of Fame! That's like being in a museum for being super awesome at soccer!

One of her most memorable tournaments was the 2019 World Cup. Alex was a leader on and off the field, scoring crucial goals and inspiring her teammates to play their best. They won the championship, and Alex celebrated with her famous tea-sipping goal celebration!

Alex Morgan isn't just a legend because of her goals and awards. She's a legend because she stands up for equal rights and shows everyone that girls can do anything boys can do in sports. She's a role model for kids everywhere who dream big and work hard to make their dreams come true. Alex Morgan is a true soccer legend, and her journey is a story of hard work, determination, and always believing in yourself!

Morgan Fun Facts

★ Young Olympian: Alex Morgan made her Olympic debut at the London 2012 Olympics, where she scored a game-winning goal against Canada in the semifinals.

★ Hat-Trick Heroine: She scored her first international hat-trick (three goals in one game) against Guatemala in 2012 during Olympic qualifying.

★ Author: Alex Morgan co-authored a series of middle-grade books called *The Kicks,* inspired by her own experiences playing soccer.

★ Fashionista: Off the field, Alex Morgan is known for her sense of style and has been featured in various fashion magazines.

★ Advocate: She is a vocal advocate for gender equality in sports and has been involved in campaigns promoting equal pay for female athletes.

★ Bilingual: Alex is fluent in Spanish, which she picked up from her Argentinian mother and Spanish-speaking family members.

★ Acting Spirit: Alongside her soccer career, Alex has launched her own movie called *Alex & Me*, which focuses on promoting positive messages and empowerment for young girls.

What Did We Learn?

★ Start Small, Dream Big: Just like Alex Morgan, start playing soccer wherever you can—whether it's in your backyard, at school, or with friends. Every great soccer journey begins with a small kick and a big dream!

★ Bounce Back from Setbacks: When things don't go your way, don't give up! Like Alex, use setbacks as opportunities to learn and come back even stronger in your game. Every challenge you overcome makes you better.

★ Break Stereotypes: Soccer is for everyone! Don't let anyone tell you otherwise. Whether you're a boy or a girl, show everyone that skill and passion have no gender. Alex Morgan proves that girls can shine just as brightly on the field.

★ Play with Heart and Joy: Feel the thrill of soccer just like Alex does. Whether you're practicing dribbling, passing, or scoring goals, play with passion and joy. Soccer is about having fun and embracing every moment on the field.

Morgan Soccer Star Quiz

Are you ready to test your knowledge about the amazing Alex Morgan? She's not just a soccer superstar but also a Disney lover, author, and advocate for equality in sports. Get ready to dive into this fun quiz and see how much you know about Alex's journey from kicking off her soccer career at a young age to scoring goals on the world stage. Let's

106

kick off this trivia and celebrate one of the most inspiring players in women's soccer history!

★ At what age did Alex Morgan start playing soccer?
  ○ a) 3 years old
  ○ b) 5 years old
  ○ c) 7 years old
  ○ d) 10 years old

★ In which year did Alex Morgan score her first international hat-trick?
- ○ a) 2009
- ○ b) 2012
- ○ c) 2015
- ○ d) 2018

★ Which college did Alex Morgan play for during her NCAA career?
- ○ a) University of North Carolina
- ○ b) Stanford University
- ○ c) University of California, Berkeley
- ○ d) University of Florida

★ How many goals did Alex Morgan score during the 2019 FIFA Women's World Cup?
- ○ a) 3 goals
- ○ b) 5 goals
- ○ c) 7 goals
- ○ d) 10 goals

★ What is the name of Alex Morgan's dog?
- ○ a) Max
- ○ b) Buddy
- ○ c) Blue
- ○ d) Rocky

★ Besides soccer, what other sport does Alex Morgan enjoy playing?
- ○ a) Basketball
- ○ b) Tennis
- ○ c) Surfing
- ○ d) Golf

★ What is the title of the middle-grade book series co-authored by Alex Morgan?
- ○ a) Kickin' It with Alex
- ○ b) The Kicks
- ○ c) Alex's Adventures in Soccer
- ○ d) Goal Scorer: The Alex Morgan Story

★ In which Olympic Games did Alex Morgan make her debut?
- ○ a) Beijing 2008
- ○ b) London 2012
- ○ c) Rio 2016
- ○ d) Tokyo 2020

★ What is one of Alex Morgan's advocacy focuses outside of soccer?
- ○ a) Environmental conservation
- ○ b) Gender equality in sports
- ○ c) Animal welfare
- ○ d) Space exploration

Bonus Game: Alex Morgan Scavenger Hunt

Are you ready to go on an exciting scavenger hunt to learn cool things about Alex Morgan? In this scavenger hunt, you'll dive into Alex's world to uncover fun and fascinating facts about her life and career. Get ready to solve clues, search for answers, and discover what makes Alex Morgan such an inspiring athlete. Are you up for the challenge? Let's go on this journey together and celebrate the greatness of Alex Morgan!

Instructions:

1. Prepare Clues: Write clues or questions that lead participants to discover specific fun facts about Alex Morgan.
   - For example:
     - "Find out how old Alex Morgan was when she started playing soccer. Hint: It's between the ages of 4 and 6!"
     - "Discover which year Alex Morgan scored her first international hat-trick."
2. Scavenger Hunt Items: Prepare a list of items related to Alex Morgan's life and career, such as:
   - Age when she started playing soccer
   - Number of goals scored in a significant game or tournament
   - Title of the book series she authored
   - Year she made her Olympic debut
   - Any interesting hobbies or interests she has outside of soccer
3. Set the Scene: Organize the scavenger hunt in a space where participants can search for answers. This could be in a classroom,

outdoor area, or virtually using online resources.

4. Gather and Talk: After completing the scavenger hunt, gather participants to discuss the answers and share interesting facts they learned about Alex Morgan. Encourage them to share any additional fun facts they know or find inspiring about her.

This activity encourages active learning and engagement while allowing participants to discover interesting facts about Alex Morgan in a fun and interactive way.

Conclusion

"Well, there you have it," the coach said with a smile. "We learned about three great soccer players and how their stories can inspire us to be better players and better people."

Max and Emily sat cross-legged on the lush green soccer field, the warm sun casting a golden hue over their faces as they listened intently to the coach. He had just finished telling them about four amazing soccer players, Messi, Ronaldo, Mbappé, and Alex Morgan and how their stories were full of inspiration.

Max turned to Emily, excitement lighting up his eyes. "Hey, Emily, did you remember how we learned that Messi used to be really short when he was young? But he never let that stop him from becoming one of the greatest players ever!"

Emily nodded eagerly. "Yeah, and Ronaldo had to work super hard to become strong and fast. He didn't give up even when people doubted him. Plus, Alex Morgan taught us that girls soccer players can do anything that guys can do!"

The coach overheard their conversation and joined in. "That's right, guys! Messi, Ronaldo, Mbappé, and Morgan... They all faced challenges, just like we do. But they showed us that with determination and hard work, we can achieve our goals."

Max frowned slightly. "But coach, sometimes I worry that I'm not good enough to play like them. They're so amazing, and we're just kids."

The coach smiled reassuringly. "You know what? Even Messi, Ronaldo, Mbappé, and Morgan were kids once, just like you. They had to practice and learn from their mistakes. That's how they got better."

Emily added thoughtfully, "I also get scared sometimes, coach. What if I get hurt playing soccer?"

The coach nodded understandingly. "Injuries are a part of sports, Emily. But soccer also teaches us to be strong and resilient. Just like these players, we learn to get back up and keep going, no matter what."

Max spoke up again, a determined look on his face. "And I don't like it when people say soccer is only for boys. Girls can play just as well!"

The coach nodded enthusiastically. "Absolutely, Max! Soccer is for everyone who loves the game. Messi, Ronaldo, Mbappé, and Morgan... They inspire both boys and girls around the world to follow their dreams."

Emily smiled. "And I love reading about soccer, but some books don't show how exciting it really is."

The coach chuckled. "You're right, Emily. We should look for books that capture the thrill of the game and show players of all backgrounds and abilities."

As they sat on the field, the sun began to set, and Max, Emily, and the coach felt inspired. They knew that Messi, Ronaldo, Mbappé, and Morgan weren't just soccer players… They were role models who showed them the power of passion, perseverance, and believing in themselves.

"And remember," The coach said as they packed up to go home, "whether you're playing on a big field or practicing in your backyard, you're making your own soccer story every day. Just like Messi, Ronaldo, Mbappé, and Morgan did."

Then, the coach looked at Max's injury. "How are you feeling?"

Max grinned broadly, wiggling his ankle a bit. "Much better, coach! Thanks for asking. I iced it like you said, and it feels almost back to normal."

"That's great to hear," The coach said warmly, patting Max on the back. "Remember, taking care of yourself is just as important as playing hard. Now, let's go join the other kids and have some fun!"

With that, Max, Emily, and the coach trotted over to where the rest of the team was warming up. The field buzzed with excitement as the players passed the ball, laughing and shouting encouragement to each other.

Max spotted his best friend Jake and waved enthusiastically. "Hey, Jake! Watch out for my killer moves today!"

Emily joined in, dribbling the ball skillfully as she approached the group. "You better watch out, Max! I'm going to score a goal just like Alex Morgan!"

The coach chuckled as he watched the kids play. "That's the spirit, Emily! Remember what we talked about... play hard, play fair, and most importantly, have fun!"

As the sun dipped lower in the sky, the game began in earnest. Max darted across the field, his ankle feeling strong and steady. Emily weaved through defenders with grace, channeling the spirit of her favorite soccer stars. The coach cheered them on from the sidelines, his voice echoing across the field.

The game was filled with laughter, cheers, and moments of pure excitement. Max made a daring save as goalkeeper, diving to block a shot just in time. Emily showcased her fancy footwork, dribbling past opponents like a seasoned pro.

At the final whistle the score was tied, but it didn't matter. The kids high-fived each other, their faces flushed with exhilaration. Max, Emily, and the coach walked off the field together, proud of their effort and the camaraderie they had shared.

"Great game, everyone!" The coach called out, clapping his hands. "You all played like champions out there!"

Max grinned at Emily, his eyes shining with happiness. "I'm glad we talked about Messi, Ronaldo, Mbappé, and Morgan today. They really inspire me to never give up and always give my best."

Emily nodded in agreement. "Yeah, and it's awesome that we all get to play soccer together. Boys, girls, it doesn't matter. Soccer is for everyone who loves it!"

The coach smiled, his heart full as he watched his team walk off the field, laughing and talking animatedly. He knew that today wasn't just about playing soccer... it was about learning, growing, and most importantly, having fun with friends.

And as the sun set behind the distant hills, Max, Emily, and their teammates headed home, already looking forward to the next time they could lace up their cleats and chase their soccer dreams together.

What Did We Learn?

Now that we've finished reading this awesome book, we've learned a ton from Messi, Ronaldo, Mbappé, and Morgan!

We learned that never giving up is super important. Messi didn't let a growth hormone issue stop him from becoming a soccer superstar. His story taught us that with determination and never giving up, we can conquer any challenge that comes our way.

Ronaldo showed us the power of hard work. He started from a small place but became one of the best players ever through hard work and never giving up. His story inspires us to work hard and keep pushing ourselves to get better at whatever we love to do.

Mbappé's story taught us about following our passion. He loved soccer from a young age and showed us that when we follow what we love with joy and excitement, amazing things can happen. His journey encourages us to chase our dreams with passion and enthusiasm.

Alex Morgan taught us that dedication and perseverance are crucial. Despite facing challenges and setbacks, she never gave up on her dream of becoming a professional soccer player. Her story inspires us to stay dedicated to our goals and keep pushing forward, even when things get tough.

Another cool thing we learned is how important teamwork and leadership are. Messi, Ronaldo, Mbappé, and Morgan didn't just play well on their own—they also inspired their teams and showed great leadership on and off the field. Their teamwork teaches us that working together and supporting each other makes everyone stronger.

Messi, Ronaldo, Mbappé, and Morgan taught us about being humble and kind, even when we're really good at something. They showed us that being nice and respectful to others is just as important as being good at soccer.

So, after reading this book, we've not only learned about amazing soccer players but also important life lessons that can help us become better people too. Let's use what we've learned to chase our dreams; with determination, hard work, kindness, and always remembering to have fun!

What Can You Do Now?

Now that we've dived into the incredible stories of Messi, Ronaldo, Mbappé, and Morgan, it's time to put what we've learned into action!

First, remember Messi's determination. When you face challenges or things seem tough, don't give up! Keep practicing and trying your best, just like Messi did with his growth hormone issue.

Second, let's take a page out of Ronaldo's book and work hard at what we love. Whether it's soccer, art, or science, give it your all and never stop learning and improving. Hard work pays off, and you can achieve amazing things if you put in the effort.

Next, like Mbappé, follow your passion with excitement. Find what you love to do and go for it! Whether it's playing soccer, painting, or exploring new places, let your passion drive you to explore and learn more every day.

And finally, like Morgan, let's remember the power of dedication and perseverance. When things get tough, stay committed to your goals and keep pushing forward. Whether you're facing challenges in sports, school, or any other aspect of life, believe in yourself and keep working hard to achieve your dreams.

Another important thing we learned is teamwork and leadership. Just like Messi, Ronaldo, Mbappé, and Morgan, we can all be leaders and team players in our own way. Help out your friends, listen to others, and work together to achieve great things.

Lastly, let's be kind and humble, just like our soccer heroes. Treat everyone with respect and kindness, whether you're on the field, in school, or at home. Being a good person is just as important as being good at something.

So, here's your challenge: Pick one thing you've learned from Messi, Ronaldo, Mbappé, or Morgan and try it out this week. Whether it's practicing harder, helping a friend, or following your passion, take action and see how it makes a difference in your life!

Remember, you're never too young to start making a positive impact and chasing your dreams.

Let's go out there, have fun, and be awesome, just like Messi, Ronaldo, Mbappé, and Morgan!

Are you ready to take on the challenge? Let's do this!

Reflection Questions

1. Which soccer player's story inspired you the most—Messi, Ronaldo, Mbappé, or Morgan? Why?

2. What did you learn about perseverance from Messi's story? Can you think of a time when you had to persevere in your own life?

3. Morgan worked really hard to become a great soccer player. What are some things you work hard at, and how does it make you feel when you see improvement?

4. Mbappé followed his passion for soccer from a young age. What are you passionate about, and how do you pursue it?

5. How do you think teamwork and leadership are important in soccer, based on what you read about Messi, Ronaldo, Mbappé, and Morgan?

6. Messi faced challenges with a growth hormone deficiency. What challenges have you faced, and how did you overcome them?

7. Ronaldo came from a small island and became a global soccer star. What dreams do you have for your future, and what steps can you take to achieve them?

8. Mbappé won the World Cup at a young age. How do you think winning such a big event changed his life?

9. What qualities do Messi, Ronaldo, Mbappé, and Morgan have that make them good role models for kids like you?

10. How did reading about Messi, Ronaldo, Mbappé, and Morgan make you feel about playing soccer or other sports?

11. In what ways are Messi, Ronaldo, Mbappé and Morgan similar? How are they different?

12. What surprised you the most about Messi's, Ronaldo's, Mbappé's, or Morgan's life story?

13. If you could ask Messi, Ronaldo, Mbappé, or Morgan one question, what would it be?

14. How do you think Messi, Ronaldo, Mbappé, and Morgan's childhood experiences shaped who they are as soccer players today?

15. Which moment from Messi's, Ronaldo's, Mbappé's, or Morgan's career would you like to witness in person? Why?

16. How do you think Messi, Ronaldo, Mbappé, and Morgan use their fame to make a positive impact on others?

17. What advice would Messi, Ronaldo, Mbappé, or Morgan give to kids who want to become soccer players?

18. Which soccer skill of Messi's, Ronaldo's, Mbappé's, or Morgan's would you like to learn and why?

19. How can you apply the lessons you learned from Messi, Ronaldo, Mbappé's, and Morgan's stories in your own life?

20. What did you find most inspiring about Messi's, Ronaldo's, Mbappé's, or Morgan's journey to success?

These questions are designed to help you think deeper about the stories you've read and how they can inspire you in your own life. Have fun reflecting!

Thank You

Thank you for joining me on this exciting journey through the lives of Messi, Ronaldo, Mbappé, and Morgan! I hope you've learned valuable lessons about perseverance, hard work, following your passion, teamwork, leadership, and kindness.

I also hope you had a blast diving into the world of soccer with these amazing players. Whether you're a soccer fanatic or just discovering the sport, their stories show us that with dedication and determination, anything is possible.

So, keep practicing your skills, chasing your dreams, and being kind to others. Remember, you can achieve greatness just like Messi, Ronaldo, Mbappé, and Morgan by believing in yourself and never giving up.

Keep playing, keep learning, and most importantly, keep having fun! Until next time, stay inspired and keep kicking those goals!

Chapter "Good Will"

Research has shown that helping others without expecting anything in return can lead to increased happiness and satisfaction in life. In today's reading or listening experience, I would like to give you the opportunity to experience that same feeling. All it requires is a few moments of your time to answer a simple question:

Would you be willing to make a difference in the life of someone you have never met without spending any money or seeking recognition for your good deeds?

If your answer is yes, then I have a small request for you. If you have found value in your reading or listening experience today, I humbly ask that you take a brief moment right now to leave an honest review of this book. It will only take 30 seconds of your time - just a few seconds to share your thoughts with others.

Your feedback can help someone else discover the same inspiration and knowledge that you have gained from this book. If you are unsure of how to leave a review for a Kindle or e-reader book, it is quite simple:

If you have a physical copy of this book, you can find the book page on Amazon (or wherever you purchased it) and leave your review there.

If you are reading on Kindle or an e-reader, simply scroll to the last page of the book and swipe up. The review prompt should appear.

Join the Adventure with "Inspirational Soccer Stories for Kids Series"

Hey there, champions of tomorrow! I've got something special for you. If you loved the journey we've been on together, then you're in for a treat. The adventure doesn't have to end here—not when there are so many more stories to be told and heroes to meet!

If you're hungry for more tales of triumph, teamwork, and the magic of soccer, then you've got to check out my book series, "Inspirational Soccer Stories for Kids." It's packed with the kind of stories that make you want to lace up your cleats and hit the field, dreaming of your own soccer glory.

And guess what? There's one book that I'm super excited for you — **"The Soccer Legends Activity Book for Smart Boys and Girls aged 6-12."** With this activity book, every page is designed to spark creativity and ignite a passion for the game. Whether your child is in the mood to doodle or learn more about their beloved game, this book offers HOURS of soccer-themed, gadget-free fun while promoting cognitive development and sportsmanship.

So, what are you waiting for? The whistle's blown, and it's time to get the ball rolling. Grab a copy, snuggle up, and get ready to be inspired all over again. Because in the world of soccer, every day is a chance to be inspired, to learn, and to become the legend you're meant to be.

Let's keep the dream alive, team. See you on the next page!

If you want to learn more about Inspirational Soccer Book for Kids and the Soccer Legends, please check out my Author Profile on Amazon here.

Answer Key

Messi Soccer Star Quiz

Answers:

1. a) Lionel Andrés Messi
2. a) FC Barcelona
3. c) 7
4. c) 2005
5. a) 7
6. b) Argentina
7. d) Forward
8. b) UEFA Champions League Top Scorer
9. a) Antonella Roccuzzo
10. c) 3

Bonus Game: Messi Match

Answers:

1. (h)
2. (d)
3. (g)
4. (e)
5. (j)
6. (b)
7. (f)
8. (i)
9. (c)
10. (a)

Ronaldo Soccer Star Quiz

1. b) Cristiano Ronaldo dos Santos Aveiro
2. c) 7
3. b) 2002
4. a) Manchester United
5. a) 7
6. b) 5
7. b) Portugal
8. a) CR7
9. a) Right
10. a) Juventus

Bonus Game: Ronaldo's Fun Fill-in-the-Blank Adventure!

Cristiano Ronaldo was born on February 5, 1985, in Funchal, Madeira, Portugal.

As a kid, Ronaldo loved playing **soccer** in the streets with his friends.

Ronaldo joined Sporting Clube de Portugal's youth academy at the age of **12**.

In **2002**, Ronaldo made his professional debut for Sporting CP's first team.

In **2003**, Ronaldo signed with Manchester United and became known for his incredible **speed** and **dribbling skills**.

Ronaldo won his first FIFA Ballon d'Or award in **2008**, while playing for **Manchester United**.

In **2009**, Ronaldo transferred to Real Madrid for a world-record fee at that time of **94** million euros.

Ronaldo helped Real Madrid win **4** Champions League titles during his time at the club.

In **2018**, Ronaldo joined Juventus and continued to showcase his talent in **Italy**.

Cristiano Ronaldo has represented his national team, Portugal, in numerous international tournaments, including the FIFA World Cup and UEFA **European** Championship.

Mbappé Soccer Star Quiz

1. B) 6 years old
2. A) AS Monaco
3. B) 17 years old
4. C) 2018
5. D) 22 years old
6. B) 3 seasons
7. A) Barcelona
8. A) Football coach
9. A) Luxembourg
10. A) Youngest French goalscorer in World Cup history

Bonus Game: Mbappé Word Search Adventure

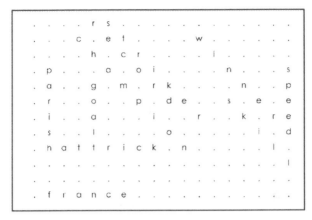

Word directions and start points are formatted: (Direction, X, Y)

hat-trick (E,2,9)
champion (SE,4,2)
striker (SE,6,1)
france (E,2,12)

winner (SE,12,2)
record (SE,5,1)
speed (S,18,4)
paris (S,2,4)

skill (SE,14,6)
goal (S,5,5)

Morgan Soccer Star Quiz

1. b) 5 years old
2. b) 2012
3. c) University of California, Berkeley
4. a) 3 goals
5. b) Cinderella
6. c) Blue
7. c) Surfing
8. b) The Kicks
9. b) London 2012
10. b) Gender equality in sports

References

- "60 Motivational Lionel Messi Quotes to Get You Pumped." Addicted2Success, www.addicted2success.com/quotes/60-motivational-lionel-messi-quotes-to-get-you-pumped/.
- Britannica. (n.d.). Alex Morgan. In Encyclopaedia Britannica. Retrieved June 25, 2024, from https://www.britannica.com/biography/Alex-Morgan
- Biography.com Editors. "Cristiano Ronaldo." Biography.com, A&E Television Networks, 17 Feb. 2021, www.biography.com/athlete/cristiano-ronaldo.
- Biography.com Editors. "Lionel Messi." Biography.com, A&E Television Networks, 22 Sep. 2021, https://www.biography.com/athletes/lionel-messi.
- BrainyQuote. "Cristiano Ronaldo Quotes." BrainyQuote, www.brainyquote.com/authors/cristiano-ronaldo-quotes.
- "Cristiano Ronaldo." Britannica, www.britannica.com/biography/Cristiano-Ronaldo.
- Encyclopædia Britannica. (n.d.). Kylian Mbappé. In Encyclopædia Britannica online. Retrieved June 25, 2024, from

https://www.britannica.com/biography/Kylian-Mbappe

- "FIFA." FIFA, www.fifa.com/en/watch/6blqEzFNBrhivdPbPy3Ccn.
- FIFA. (2023, December 18). Kylian Mbappé profile - The Best FIFA Football Awards 2023. FIFA. Retrieved June 25, 2024, from https://www.fifa.com/en/the-best-fifa-football-awards/articles/kylian-mbappe-profile-the-best-2023
- Girls Soccer Network. (2017, April 10). 13 things you didn't know about Alex Morgan. Retrieved June 25, 2024, from https://girlssoccernetwork.com/13-things-didnt-know-alex-morgan/
- Goal. (n.d.). 13 fun facts about Kylian Mbappé. Goal. Retrieved June 25, 2024, from https://www.goal.com/en-us/lists/13-fun-facts-about-kylian-mbappe/blt3723d57468a6b53c
- Goal. (2023, October 4). Kylian Mbappé car collection: Volkswagen, Ferrari, and more. Goal. Retrieved June 25, 2024, from https://www.goal.com/en-us/news/kylian-mbappe-car-collection-volkswagen-ferrari/blt97a1193def3658ec
- IMDb. (n.d.). Alex Morgan. IMDb. Retrieved June 25, 2024, from https://www.imdb.com/title/tt8179218/
- IPL.org. "The Challenges of Ronaldo's Life in Soccer." IPL.org, www.ipl.org/essay/The-

Challenges-Of-Ronaldos-Life-In-Soccer-PCYDZQ3RU.

- Levs, J. (2013, June 13). Girl Rising: Alex Morgan. CNN. Retrieved June 25, 2024, from https://www.cnn.com/2013/06/13/world/girl-rising-alex-morgan/index.html
- "Lionel Messi Isn't Just a Good Player; He's Also a Good Human." The Media Line, 26 Dec. 2022, themedialine.org/mideast-mindset/lionel-messi-isnt-just-a-good-player-hes-also-a-good-human/.
- "Lionel Messi's 'Warm-Up' Playlist Features Bad Bunny, Peso Pluma, Karol G, Grupo Frontera & More." Billboard, Billboard-Hollywood Reporter Media Group, 21 February 2024, https://www.billboard.com/music/latin/lionel-messi-playlist-soccer-stars-favorite-songs-1235611454/.
- National Today. (n.d.). Kylian Mbappé's birthday: Facts & celebration. National Today. Retrieved June 25, 2024, from https://nationaltoday.com/birthday/kylian-mbappe/
- No Grass in the Clouds. "Does Lionel Messi Have a Limit?" No Grass in the Clouds, 2024, nograssintheclouds.substack.com/p/does-lionel-messi-have-a-limit.
- Real Madrid Official Website. "Cristiano Ronaldo Dos Santos Aveiro." Real Madrid, www.realmadrid.com/en-US/the-

club/history/football-legends/cristiano-ronaldo-dos-santos-aveiro

- Sportskeeda. "Ronaldo Family." Sportskeeda, www.sportskeeda.com/football/ronaldo-family.
- Super Teacher Worksheets. (n.d.). Homepage. Super Teacher Worksheets. Retrieved June 25, 2024, from https://www.superteacherworksheets.com/
- "The Titans Football Academy." The Titans Football Academy, n.d., thetitansfa.com/football-messi-skills-mastery-guide/#:~
- =Lionel%20Messi's%20style%20of%20play,him%20apart%20from%20other%20players.
- UEFA. (n.d.). Kylian Mbappé: Goals, records, stats, and claims to fame. UEFA. Retrieved June 25, 2024, from https://www.uefa.com/uefachampionsleague/news/026d-13576e235a82-2cfb6b06ef27-1000--kylian-mbappe-goals-records-stats-and-claims-to-fame-how-bri/
- Ultra Football. (n.d.). The story of Kylian Mbappé. Ultra Football. Retrieved June 25, 2024, from https://www.ultrafootball.com/blogs/ultra-mag/the-story-of-kylian-mbappe
- Wattpad. (n.d.). Facts about football players: Alex Morgan. Retrieved June 25, 2024, from https://www.wattpad.com/266705859-facts-about-football-players-alex-morgan

Made in United States
Troutdale, OR
12/03/2024